THE INTERNATIONAL BUSINESS TRAVELER'S COMPANION

THE INTERNATIONAL BUSINESS TRAVELER'S COMPANION

Donald Eulette deKieffer

INTERCULTURAL PRESS

For information, contact:
Intercultural Press, Inc.
P.O. Box 700
Yarmouth, Maine 04096, USA

Book design by Jacques Chauzaud
Book production by Patty Topel
Cover design by Letterspace
Illustrations by Don Herberg Okazaki

Printed in the United States of America.

97 96 95 94 93 92   1 2 3 4 5 6

Library of Congress Cataloging-in-Publication Data

deKieffer, Donald Eulette
    The international business traveler's companion / Donald Eulette deKieffer.
        p. cm.
    Includes bibliographical references
    ISBN 1-877864-12-9
    1. Business travel—Handbooks, manuals, etc. I. Title.
G156.5.B86D45   1992
910'.2'02—dc20   92-34504
                                                            CIP

DEDICATION

To Nancy, who vicariously endured many of the disasters
which inspired this book.

ACKNOWLEDGMENTS

Without the gracious assistance of more than three score traveling business executives, this book could not have been written. Out
of deference to their privacy, I will not link their humiliating experiences to them by name—unless, of course, they are nominated to
become the Secretary of State.

WARNING:

Certain information contained in this book relates to U.S. government regulations. As far as the author and publisher are aware, the information is accurate as of the date of publication. Neither the author nor the publisher, however, make any representations about the accuracy or thoroughness of the information contained herein. Readers are strongly advised to contact relevant government agencies concerning current restrictions and regulations. Telephone numbers and addresses are contained both in the bibliography and throughout the text of this book. The reader should be aware, however, that the government addresses and telephone numbers are subject to change without notice. Be sure you have up-to-date information before you engage in any international travel or commercial transactions.

1992 Donald Eulette deKieffer

Contents

The Secretary of Commerce
Washington, D.C. 20230

Dear International Business Traveler:

The future of American commerce is tightly linked with international trade. The United States is already the preeminent trading country in the world. To remain so, American business executives will have to travel abroad with increasing frequency.

Information such as that contained in *The International Business Traveler's Companion* should help make overseas business trips successful. Of particular usefulness is information on the assistance available to business executives from various sources, including the U.S. Government, and instruction to executives on how to work effectively with these sources.

Business travelers who fail to seek such assistance—for example, from the Department of Commerce's U.S. and Foreign Commercial Service—may be placing themselves at a competitive disadvantage. To remain strong in the world market, I encourage the international business executive to become informed of the available sources of help and support. In particular, I urge you to take advantage of the international trade services and programs offered by the Department of Commerce.

Sincerely,

Robert A. Mosbacher

Introduction

Every year, millions of business executives travel abroad to promote their products or represent their companies. These trips can be, and often are, disasters. Luggage gets lost and the executive shows up at the first meeting in jogging shoes and a sweatshirt. Hotel reservations are lost; appointments are missed. Negotiations flounder on the reefs of language. Customers are insulted by the bizarre behavior of the visitor. And, in a few cases, the executive becomes the guest of the local constabulary.

The International Business Traveler's Companion is designed to help executive voyagers through the minefields of overseas business travel. It is *not* a "country-specific" guide like most other reference books, but rather provides generic advice which can be used in any situation. No one reference can cover all the topics which an executive needs when traveling overseas, and readers are urged to consult the many sources scattered throughout this book and in the bibliography for country-specific (and issue-specific) advice.

This book was written as a result of hundreds of mistakes made by the author, his colleagues, and acquaintances. The problems identified herein are real, having been discussed in vivid detail in hotel bars from Singapore to São Paulo. It is hoped that those who read this guide and heed its content will be able to listen to similar stories, secure in the knowledge that those things won't happen to them.

Nevertheless, I recognize that there are adventures in travel I have not even dreamed of, and I earnestly solicit war stories. If you have one, or even want to comment on what is written here, please write to Intercultural Press, PO Box 700, Yarmouth, ME 04096, USA. Your experience may be incorporated into future editions.

Supply Checklist for Business Travel Overseas

TRAVEL AND FINANCIAL DOCUMENTS

Passport: valid for at least three months after the date of your expected return (*see chapter 1*)

Visas (*see chapter 1*)

Tickets, hotel confirmations, car rental reservations

Cash, traveler's checks (*see chapter 3*)

Records of the serial numbers of your traveler's checks: store separately

Credit cards: leave local cards at home; take only major, internationally accepted credit cards (AMEX, Diners Club, VISA, MasterCard, telephone charge cards, etc.) (*see chapter 3*)

Driver's license (*see chapter 13*)

International driving permit (*see chapter 13*)

Photocopies of important documents:

- driver's license
- airline tickets
- passport identification pages
- credit card numbers
- travel itinerary

Frequent flyer cards (see chapter 2)

Customs certificates of registration/carnets (see chapters 1 and 16)

International Certificate of Vaccination (see chapter 1)

Medical card: this should contain names, addresses, and telephone numbers of your personal physician, information on any medical conditions you have, and details concerning (U.S.) medical insurance *(see chapter 10)*

Passport photos (see chapter 1)

BUSINESS EQUIPMENT

Business cards (see chapter 12)

Laptop computer: connector wires, acoustic coupler *(see chapter 12)*

Dictating machine

Pocket calendar

Hand-held calculator

Supplies:
- Scotch tape
- paper clips
- stapler, extra staples, staple remover
- batteries and cassettes for dictating equipment
- formatted floppy disks
- stationery/letterhead
- envelopes
- preaddressed (international), postage prepaid air express plastic envelopes
- corporate and personal checkbooks
- two small manila or plastic envelopes for receipts

- writing instruments, highlighters, etc.
- rubber bands

TRAVEL SUPPLIES

Guidebooks and maps (see chapter 12)

Foreign language phrase book/dictionary

Camera/film

Converter plugs/transformer (see chapter 12)

Travel alarm clock (see chapter 12)

Portable shortwave radio

Flashlight

Swiss army knife (see chapter 4)

First-aid kit (see chapter 4)

Money belt (see chapter 4)

Door lock

Opaque plastic bag (see chapter 4)

Ziploc storage bags for currency and for aerosol cans (see chapters 3 and 4)

Collapsible umbrella

Immersion heater (see chapter 4)

Dop kit (see chapter 4)

Cigarettes (for smokers): U.S.-made cigarettes cost twice as much overseas

Gifts (see chapter 12)

Things to Do before Departure

1. Get a passport (*see chapter 1*).
2. Check with the embassy of the country(ies) you intend to visit to determine the visa and customs requirements, and apply as necessary (*see chapter 1*).
3. Purchase a carnet if appropriate (*see chapter 1*).
4. Check with the State Department to determine if travel advisories are in effect (*see chapter 11*).
5. Get recommended inoculations and International Certificate of Vaccination (*see chapter 1*).
6. If you have a physical disability or a medication which requires special storage facilities, contact your hotel(s) to ensure that your needs can be met.
7. Leave copies of important documents—medical and dental records, serial numbers of traveler's checks, travel itinerary, airline ticket, credit cards, first two pages of your passport, and driver's license—with your family or office. Take another set with you.
8. Put your personal affairs in order: wills, guardianship ar-

rangements, etc. Tell your family or office where they can find personal documents.

9. Check your personal and company insurance policies to determine if coverage is adequate for your journey.

10. Purchase any guidebooks, foreign language phrase books, or other resources you plan to take with you.

11. If you are planning on carrying firearms overseas, check with the relevant airline(s) for their transport procedures (*see chapter 5*). For overseas licensing requirements, *see chapter 1*.

12. Obtain an international driver's permit (*see chapter 13*). Make sure your regular driver's license will remain valid throughout your trip.

13. Get four 2x2 pictures in addition to the two you need for your passport (*see chapter 1*).

14. Obtain a letter of certification from your physician for any medication which requires a prescription, especially if it contains a narcotic (*see chapter 4*).

15. Register particularly valuable items (watches, firearms, etc.), especially if they are new and are of foreign origin, with the U.S. Customs Service (*see chapter 12*).

16. Put your name and address inside each piece of luggage you will be taking.

17. Prepare and laminate a card which includes the name, address, and telephone number of your personal physician, insurance company, family, and business contact; your passport number and place of issuance; and frequent flyer numbers. This card should be carried with you at all times.

1

Travel Documents

OBTAINING A PASSPORT

To apply for a passport for the first time, you must present, in person, an application at a State Department Passport Agency. These are located in many major cities in federal and state courthouses and United States post offices authorized to accept passport applications (see appendix 5 for a list of U. S. State Department passport agencies). Application forms (officially titled DSP-11) may be requested by mail in advance, or obtained at the agency. Your completed application must be accompanied by proof of U.S. citizenship (i.e., birth certificate, naturalization certificate, certificate of citizenship, or Consular Report of Birth) and two 2x2 photographs, either in color or black and white. The fee is $42, and the passport is valid for ten years for adults and five years for children under eighteen.

If you have no birth certificate, you may send a baptismal certificate, a hospital birth record, or secondary evidence such as school, census, Bible, or insurance records. If you do not have any of these documents, you may present yourself at a passport office with someone who has known you for at least two years. He or she will be required to sign an affidavit regarding your status. Proof of your identity as a U.S. citizen is *not* established by a Social Security card, a temporary driver's license, a credit card, or any temporary, altered, or expired identification.

You can expect to receive your new passport in approximately two weeks. Make sure to allow ample time for mail delays; it is a good idea to apply no later than two months prior to your departure date.

If your passport was issued within twelve years prior to the date of a new application, you can renew it through the mail by picking up an application at U.S. post offices or at a passport agency. The mail procedure costs about $35 and can take up to four weeks during the spring and summer travel seasons.

The passport office accepts bank drafts, certified or personal checks, traveler's checks, or money orders. Cash is accepted if you go to the passport office in person but should not be sent through the mail.

If you already have a passport, check to ensure that it will be valid for at least three months beyond the date you expect to return. Some countries will issue visas only in passports which are valid for a year beyond the date of the issuance of the visa. Further, if you return to the United States with an expired passport, you will be subject to a passport waiver fee of $80, payable to the Immigration and Naturalization Service at the port of entry.

For the business traveler, it is well worth a few extra dollars to get a forty-eight-page passport, which has more pages for visas and entry and exit stamps than the normal twenty-four-page passport. If you fill your passport with stamps well before its expiration date, you can have additional pages inserted by the passport office without charge.

Before departing on any international trip, you should make several photocopies of the first two pages of your passport. One copy should be given to family members at home, and one should be on file at your office. Take a third copy with you, and carry it separately from your actual passport in case it is lost or stolen.

For a free pamphlet, passport application, and passport renewal, contact the public affairs staff at the Bureau of Consular Affairs, Room 5807, U.S. Department of State, Washington, D.C. 20520. Additional questions can be directed to the local U.S. State Department Passport Agency or to the headquarters in Washington, D.C. (tel. (202) 647-0518).

DOUBLE PASSPORTS AND "BLIND" VISAS

Many African and Middle Eastern countries will deny entry if visa stamps from Israel, Taiwan, or South Africa appear in your passport. The embassies of these countries can tell you in advance if this will be a problem. The State Department Passport Agency sometimes permits you to have a second passport in these circumstances, or will issue "blind visas" on plain paper rather than stamping them on your passport. It is a good idea to request these services if they are available. To find out about current restrictions, call the State Department Citizens Emergency Center at (202) 647-5225.

VISAS

Not all countries require visas for entry, and, fortunately, those that do are relaxing their requirements considerably. It is now much easier for a business traveler to go from country to country without long waits to secure the necessary entry documents. Nevertheless, visa requirements change rapidly, and you should always check current regulations before attempting to enter a country. The Department of State publication, *Foreign Visa Requirements*, contains entry information for individual countries and is available from the Consumer Information Center, Department 438T, Pueblo, CO 81009. The U.S. State Department Citizens' Emergency Center also provides information on visa requirements of foreign governments (tel. (202) 647-5225).

OBTAINING A VISA

There are three ways to obtain a visa: through visa services, at the border, and through the mail.

1. Visa services.

Located in Washington, D.C. are a number of visa services, which will take care of all the hassles of procuring a visa. They will send you the necessary documents as well as instructions for filling them out. You then return the completed forms along with your passport, a check, and pictures as necessary. They will take care of the details and mail your passport to you with the appropriate visa(s). Allow at least ten days (or longer if so instructed by the visa service) to get your visa in this manner. Visa service charges range from $25-$50 per visa *plus* fees charged by the embassy for the visa. Be sure and inquire in advance about these. For a listing of popular visa services, see appendix 7.

2. At the airport.

Some countries allow foreigners to purchase "border visas" upon entry to their country. This is literally a last-minute procedure and should be used only in an emergency. The consular office of the country you intend to visit will know if this method is available. Also find out if the airport visa office will be open at the time your flight arrives; otherwise, you may have to spend hours waiting in a transit hall for your visa to be issued. Border visas are usually available only at major entry points, such as airports, and not at many other border crossings.

3. Through the mail.

Procuring your own visa is not a complicated process, and doing so can often save time and money. Call or write the foreign embassy or consulate nearest you, ask about visa requirements, obtain a form, and send it to the appropriate office. Visa requirements change, so consult the consulate before each trip. For a partial list of foreign embassies and chanceries in the United States, see appendix 4.

Some countries only issue single or limited-duration entry visas. Try to get the longest duration you can, with as many entries as possible. This may be somewhat more expensive, but in the long run it will be less time-consuming than securing separate visas for each trip.

NOTE: If you are applying for any type of visa through the mail, it is always a good idea to include a letter containing specific instructions in addition to the required photos, forms, and payment. *Make sure to specify the date you are departing from your home country.*

TRANSIT VISAS

A transit visa is a document which you may need to acquire even if you are not stopping in a particular country. This visa allows you to pass through a country en route to your destination, even if you don't plan to get off the plane. Check with the State Department's Citizens Emergency Center (tel. (202) 647-5225) for information on transit visa requirements.

TOURIST CARDS

In some countries short-term visitors are required to carry a tourist card instead of or in addition to a visa. Tourist cards are usually easier to obtain than visas; you can generally get one from the country's embassy or consulate, from an airline serving the country, or at the port of entry. For some tourist cards, a fee is required. Keep your tourist card in your passport, secured with a paper clip. Some countries require that you surrender your card upon departure.

EXIT/ENTRY STAMPS

Many countries, especially in Western Europe, no longer require entry and exit stamps when you cross their borders. Even the United States is following this trend for returning citizens. Nevertheless, ask the immigration officials to stamp your passport with entry and exit dates. This provides a handy record of your overseas travel and is particularly useful if you apply for a U.S. government job which requires a security check. Remember, do *not* request that entry and exit stamps be placed in your passport for sensitive countries (see page 3, "Double Passports and 'Blind' Visas").

MEDICAL CLEARANCE

In the case of physical disability, illness, and certain other conditions, the traveler should notify travel personnel of any special requirements at the time your reservations are made. In some cases you may be required to obtain medical clearance in the form of a physician's letter certifying your ability to travel. Medical clearance is recommended or required for people who fall under the following categories:

- Those who have undergone recent surgery
- Those with an unstable physical or mental condition
- Women in late stages of pregnancy
- Anyone with a contagious disease for which quarantine is required
- Newborns (less than one week old)
- Those whose illness or disability does not permit them to take care of themselves

The requirements for a medical clearance vary according to country and airline, so check with the appropriate officials in advance.

INTERNATIONAL CERTIFICATES OF VACCINATION

An International Certificate of Vaccination, or ICV, is a document approved by the World Health Organization (WHO) and issued by the Ministry of Health of various countries (in the U.S., the Department of Health and Human Services, Office of Public Health Service). This passport-sized booklet contains a personal history of your inoculations for various diseases, including smallpox, yellow fever, cholera, typhus, typhoid, plague, polio, tetanus, etc. If you are traveling to areas where diseases are prevalent—particularly the tropics—you should have one of these documents since you may be required to show proof of inoculation upon entry into the country. Some nations now specifically require AIDS clearance in addition to the aforementioned diseases. See *chapter 10* for more information on diseases, AIDS, and inoculation.

ICVs are available from the Government Printing Office in Washington, D.C., but it is best to ask your doctor for one. Fill in your name and address on the first page, and have your physician or health service stamp it when you receive the inoculation(s). When traveling abroad, keep this with you as you enter and leave a country, then store it in a safe place (such as your hotel safe) until you depart. Remember to bring the document with you if you are hospitalized.

OTHER DOCUMENTS

In Western Europe, customs documents are no longer needed for cars temporarily imported by tourists or businesspeople. However, a customs document called a *Carnet de Passages en Douane* may be useful in some countries. A carnet is a document which lists those goods you are taking into a country which you plan to carry back out with you. Carnets are generally obtainable through automobile clubs in Europe, rental car companies, or the U.S. Council for International Business. In some countries, customs authorities demand deposits against many of your goods unless you have one of these documents. Even if you return through the same customs post, the bureaucratic delays involved in recovering these deposits are horrendous. A carnet must be properly endorsed at each frontier and, after your trip is over, returned to the issuing organization and correctly endorsed to avoid customs problems and expense. Carnets are particularly useful if you are traveling with commercial samples which are intended for demonstration purposes. Commercial carnets may be procured from the United States Council for International Business, 1212 Avenue of the Americas, New York, NY 10036-1689.

In most European countries a "green card" is essential if you intend to drive. This is an international vehicle insurance certificate. It is generally included with the other documents you will be given if you rent a car, but you should also get one if you are driving someone else's car. Be sure to sign it. If you are driving your personal vehicle, the local automobile club can assist you in procuring a green card. Contact the American Automobile Association in the U.S. before you leave to get information about foreign clubs.

Residents of the United States carrying firearms or ammunition with them to other countries should consult the customs officials of the respective embassies of those countries (as well as countries you will be stopping at in transit) as to their regulations and licensing requirements. For additional information, contact the Bureau of Alcohol, Tobacco and Firearms (ATF), Department of the Treasury, Washington, DC 20226, and the Office of Munitions Control, Department of State, Washington, DC 20520.

Also, to facilitate your reentry when you return to the U.S., have your firearms and ammunition registered before you leave at any customs office or ATF field office. However, not more than three nonautomatic weapons and 1,000 cartridges can be registered by any one person. Quantities beyond these are subject to the Export Licensing requirements of the Office of Munitions Control.

If you are considering trying to return to the U.S. with either agricultural or wild animal products, *see chapter 16* for restrictions and permits.

CUSTOMS CERTIFICATE OF REGISTRATION

Items such as watches, cameras, tape recorders, firearms, or other possessions which may be readily identified by serial number or permanently affixed markings may be taken to a U.S. Customs office nearest you and registered before your departure (see appendix 6). The Certificate of Registration will expedite free entry of these items when you return. Keep the certificate; it is valid for any future trips as long as the information on it remains legible and current. Registration cannot be processed by telephone nor can blank registration forms be given or mailed to you to fill out at a later time.

It is a good idea to contact the previously mentioned agencies, and particularly the embassies of the countries you plan to visit or travel through, with your list of questions several months before your date of departure. To summarize, this list should include the following questions:

- Are visas required? What are the procedures for acquiring a visa? How long will it take to get one, and how much will it cost?

- If your passport contains visa stamps from Israel, South Africa, or Taiwan, will entry be a problem? Are double passports or blind visas available?
- Are border visas available at the airport of arrival? At what times are airport visa offices open?
- Is a tourist card or transit visa required?
- What restrictions are there on imports into the country? Firearms? Alcohol? Political/religious material? Are there restrictions on exports?
- Are any of your goods eligible for a carnet? Will any of your goods require duty fees? Approximately how much?
- What is the procedure for procuring a green card?
- Is it permissible to import that country's currency into the country?
- Can you claim your bags and recheck them yourself if you are a transit passenger (*see chapter 2*)?
- Are there any restrictions on transmitting data via modem from the country?
- What financial data are required (proof of sufficient funds, proof of onward or return ticket)?.
- Are immunizations required? If so, which ones? Is AIDS clearance certification necessary? If you are in any way disabled or have a condition that may require medical clearance, what are the requirements?
- Is there a departure tax?

2

Travel Preparations

While some people may regard international travel as glamorous, most business executives are more interested in comfort and efficiency. Frankly, the travel element of a business trip is usually the least enjoyable part of the excursion. This chapter deals with how to make the unfortunate necessity of travel less disagreeable.

LUGGAGE

Bags rarely get lost on the way home. The gods have dictated that if a bag is to be lost, it will be done on your outward-bound trip. You will therefore be sans underwear, ties, and toiletries for two weeks while your bags are sitting in Istanbul. As veteran travelers say, "There are only two kinds of luggage—carry-on and lost." To avoid the latter type, take only carry-on luggage. This may not be possible on longer trips, but if you will be traveling for less than a week, you should be able to manage it. If you must check your luggage, at least pack a toilet kit in your carry-on bags as well as a change of clothes.

Although many business travelers prefer to dress casually in transit, it is wise to wear clothing which would be acceptable in a business context should your bags be lost.

Some airport routings are more dangerous than others when it comes to losing bags, particularly if you are changing airlines. When you are traveling long distances, allow at least three hours between flights, which guards against delays and leaves ample time to transfer your bags.

To avoid potential mix-ups, do not trust the ground crews to efficiently transfer your luggage from one airline to another. Check your bags yourself through each leg of the journey: claim them at your first transfer spot and check them for the next flight. Ordinarily, this should not require you to go through customs. Merely claim your bag and recheck it at the airline service counter. You may, however, have to clear immigration control depending upon the requirements of a particular country. You should ask the embassy of the transit country about this before leaving, particularly if that country requires a visa.

If it is not possible to claim your bag in transit, be sure there is nothing essential in the luggage you check. You can get along for a few days without clothing (if necessary, you can buy some at your final destination), but it may be impossible to do without samples, technical data, literature, etc. Anything that is a "must have" should be in your carry-on bag.

FEAR OF FLYING

Many people are terrified of getting on planes. Since international business travelers have no alternative, there are a number of things you can do to alleviate this problem. *Travel Agent Magazine* has compiled a list of resources to help those with aviaphobia overcome their sometimes paralyzing disability. If you are afflicted with fear of flying, see Other Resources for a listing of these materials and services.

JET LAG

There are as many nostrums for jet lag as there are experts in politics. Nevertheless, certain strategies seem to work for nearly everyone.

Fly business class or better. If you can afford it, always fly business or first class if possible. Sleeping on planes is difficult enough as it is. Business class seats give you slightly more room and enable you to stretch out a bit more. However, if the flight is not fully booked, it is sometimes possible to fly economy and get even more room. If this is the case, book an aisle seat in the center row in the rear of the aircraft (window and aisle seats against the bulkheads go first). If you are fortunate, you may get two, three, or even four seats to yourself and can sleep horizontally.

Don't drink too much. Although drinks are generally free in first and business class and the temptation may be great, resist the urge to indulge yourself. Alcohol causes severe dehydration. When coupled with time changes it can give you a world-class hangover for days.

Don't schedule meetings for your day of arrival. Some business travelers attempt to prove how invincible they are by going to the hotel, taking a quick shower, and going straight into a business meeting. Many companies, however, strictly forbid this practice—and for good reason. Negotiating overseas contracts is difficult enough without being giddy and exhausted. It is almost always best to relax on your first day of arrival in a foreign country and organize your presentation. Do not take a nap in the afternoon. Try to stay awake until about an hour before your usual bedtime, then go to sleep. This procedure will help you adjust to the local time zone as quickly as possible. Some business travelers find that taking a couple of aspirin and a multivitamin before and during their trips helps to prevent headaches and otherwise makes the adjustment easier. Drinking plenty of nonalcoholic liquids is also a good idea.

The above suggestions will only reduce jet lag, not eliminate it. For a comprehensive program that really works, buy a copy of *Overcoming Jet Lag*, by Ehret and Scanlon (see Bibliography). This book outlines a program including a balanced diet and regulated exercise and sleep, which has helped millions of international travelers.

FREQUENT FLYERS

Most U.S. airlines maintain frequent flyer clubs. Overseas business travelers can rack up zillions of frequent flyer miles, which can be put toward free tickets or other bonuses. While the best procedure is to fly on one airline so you can amass enough points to get free trips, this is often impractical. Join at least three or four frequent flyer clubs with American air carriers. Most of the major U.S. carriers have arrangements with foreign air carriers to transfer foreign frequent flyer points to your account, although there may be special requirements for this. Sometimes you will need to fill out a form for the foreign carrier at the airport to have your miles properly credited. Foreign carriers rarely have the ability to automatically award the air miles via computer.

Even if you have properly filled out the required forms at the airport, you should save your boarding pass and ticket receipt for at least three months after you return. If your club does not properly credit your account, these documents will demonstrate that you actually took the flight. You can send them to the American club when you receive your statement and ask that your trip be properly credited.

Have a list of your frequent flyer numbers with you at all times. Some experienced travelers have these typed on a small card and laminated for their wallet, while others prefer a credit card portfolio in which they can put frequent flyer cards, hotel cards, car rental cards, etc.

Most frequent flyer clubs offer special promotions between particular cities at various times. Before you leave, ask your travel agent or your frequent flyer club if these promotions are in effect. Often, the promotions offer double or even triple miles for travel between designated cities during specified periods. Membership in several clubs will increase your chances of coordinating your travel plans with such promotions.

If you travel often, a good source of information is *The Frequent Flyer Award Book* by John Fitzgerald and Charles Saggio (see Bibliography). For information about affinity cards, credit cards which allow you to accumulate frequent flyer miles for each dollar charged overseas, *see chapter 3,* "Affinity Cards."

TRAVEL INSURANCE

Although many insurance agencies offer extra travel insurance, these policies are generally not a good value. Air travel is so safe that the insurance company has very good odds—even on five-dollar premiums—that you'll survive the trip. In any event, your own health and life insurance should be adequate to cover you in the event of accident or death. In addition, several credit card companies provide free air travel insurance if you purchase your tickets with their card.

If you are going to be traveling to a particularly dangerous area, however, you might consider taking out a supplemental policy. Many common death and disability insurance policies have "acts of war" exclusions. This means that if you are injured or killed during a civil insurrection, those companies will not make payment. Check your policy to see if it has a clause to that effect, and get term insurance to cover the duration of your stay if it does. An independent insurance agent can generally take care of this. In extreme circumstances (e.g., lion hunting in a war zone) they may need to refer you to an international insurance broker. These policies can be rather expensive (eighty dollars per day for one million dollars of coverage in the above example).

Your employer's insurance company may also cover you. Most people do not regard going into a battle zone as a perk, and many companies will provide adequate coverage if you request it. Look into this at least a month ahead of time if possible; the wheels of the insurance industry sometimes turn slowly. Also check your health insurance coverage; policies often cover only injuries, not acquired diseases.

If you are still nervous about traveling without separate insurance coverage, see Other Resources for a list of several companies offering short-term policies for travelers.

TRAVEL BETWEEN FOREIGN COUNTRIES

If you are flying overseas to places which are not major tourist destinations, you may have difficulty securing and retaining reservations and may experience long waits at airports for customs and immigration processing. When delays are extended, make sure you are able to produce proof of a confirmed reservation to ensure that the airline will provide food and lodging. Flights are often overbooked, delayed, or canceled, and when competing for space on a plane you may be dealing with a surging crowd rather than a line. You cannot avoid all problems, but you can

- learn the reputation of the airline and airports you will use in order to anticipate problems and avoid unpleasant surprises;
- when possible, reserve your return passage before you go and reconfirm immediately upon your arrival;
- ask for written confirmation, complete with file number or locator code, when you make or confirm a reservation;
- arrive at the overseas airport earlier than required in order to put yourself in the front of the line—or the crowd, as the case may be; and
- travel with sufficient funds, in traveler's checks, for an extra week's subsistence in case you are stranded.

3

Monetary Matters

TRAVELER'S CHECKS

Travel guides traditionally tell businesspeople to carry traveler's checks. This is usually good advice. In some countries, traveler's checks get a higher rate of exchange at the official rate than does actual cash. In addition, they can be replaced if lost or stolen. If you do take traveler's checks, leave photocopies of your receipts at your office, and carry a copy with you as well, stored separately from the checks. If these receipts are lost, you will be unable to make a claim.

CASH

Cash is still a useful commodity. U.S. exchange rates are generally lower than those you can get in the country itself. Before you leave, obtain only enough foreign currency (fifty dollars or so) for transportation to town from the airport of your destination. If you are transporting declarable items, be sure you have cash to pay duty rates at customs (*see chapter 6*).

There are several advantages to carrying some cash on a business trip. In many countries, the official rate bears no reasonable relationship to the real, in other words, black market rate. Exchanges made at the official rate for personal expenses can often make a business trip prohibitively expensive. While the very name *black market* attests to its technical illegality, such services flourish because the official rates are so arbitrary. For purposes of this discussion, the black market will be referred to as the *free market.*

Often the discrepancies between the official and the free market rates are enormous. Differences of up to ten times the official rate are not uncommon. This can make daily living expenses a bargain, and many business travelers choose to take advantage of free market currencies for personal expenses. While this practice is not condoned by local authorities, it is often tolerated. There are different rates on the free market depending upon the amount of the currency you exchange. Usually the breakpoints at which these differences appear are twenty dollars and one hundred dollars. Travelers should note, however, that business transactions should never be conducted on the free market (unless there is a provision for such exchange under local law). The following are some tips for travelers who choose to deal on the free market.

Always exchange some money at the official rate, preferably at a bank at the airport upon arrival. Keep the receipt in your passport. In most countries with currency controls, you are allowed to legally reconvert local currency into hard currency if you have a receipt to demonstrate the original transaction from hard currency into local currency.

In countries with free markets, you will not have to seek the "street bankers"; they will find you. Locating free market agents is not difficult; your airport taxi driver will often be an entrepreneur and offer to exchange money. It is rarely a good idea to do so at this time, at least not until you can size up the market. Wait until you get to the hotel. One of the best ways for street bankers to find you is to take a short walk around a hotel—particularly if it is one in which foreign guests generally stay. You will be offered various rates by the local "bankers." Listen politely, but do not deal—yet. After you have been approached by four or five of these individuals, you will have a reasonable idea of the prevailing street rate. Obviously, the rate you will be offered will be below what they can get through their connections.

Dealing with street bankers can be hazardous. A favorite scam of street bankers is to conclude a deal for a large wad of local currency. They will count it out and slip it to you in exchange for your hard currency. When you check the wad of bills in your pocket later, you discover that sleight of hand is practiced all over the world. Often, the outer few bills will be genuine, while the inner portion is newspaper cut to size. There is, naturally, little you can do about this, since the transaction was probably illegal in the first place.

Exchanging your money in the hotel is a much safer procedure. Hotel restaurants are the best place to conduct free transactions in currency. Some hotel restaurants in currency-controlled countries do more business than the central banks in dollar terms. Very often you will be asked by the waiter if you wish to exchange currency. Since you know the general exchange rate from your brief encounters with their competitors on the street or in the lobby, you will have a good idea of whether the rate being offered is reasonable and is subject to negotiation. It is rare that you will be ripped off in such circumstances, since a hotel employee cannot slip out the back door with your money. This acts as a real deterrent to shortchanging. Waiters' jobs are particularly coveted in most currency-controlled countries because of the opportunities they provide.

Paying for goods and services with hard currency at free market prices is advantageous. It is possible to deal on the free market without actually exchanging any money into local currency. Often, goods and services can be paid for in hard currency at prices which reflect the free market. Such transactions are regarded as at least technically illegal in most countries with exchange controls, but at least in this case you know precisely what you are getting for your money and do not have the hassle of attempting to either reconvert or spend pocketfuls of local currency before you depart.

Beware of setups. In currency-controlled countries, local monetary authorities target businesspeople for currency transaction stings. As noted above, countries with dual markets sometimes have crimi-

nal sanctions for unapproved transactions. Local cops sometimes induce foreign businesspeople to enter into currency transactions and then arrest them, levying huge fines. *Sometimes*, the local constabulary will go so far as to assign plainclothes cops to pose as street dealers. They may actually solicit you to exchange money. The "entrapment" defense does not work in Pakistan, for example.

FOREIGN CURRENCY TRAVELER'S CHECKS

If you carry traveler's checks, it is sometimes better to have them denominated in the currency of the country in which you are traveling. U.S. dollar-denominated traveler's checks are often expensive to convert to local cash—particularly on weekends when banks are closed (and you do not get a favorable rate from your hotel). Traveler's checks are available in many Western currencies and in yen.

You can get them through American Express, the American Automobile Association, banks with foreign exchange offices, and some airline-sponsored reservation systems.

A listing of organizations which provide foreign currency traveler's checks can be found under Other Resources.

EXCESS CURRENCY

If you are traveling to more than one country, take small, Ziploc sandwich bags labeled in advance with the names of the countries you will be visiting. When you leave the country, put your spare change and small bills in these bags for your next trip; this will keep it from getting mixed up with local currency.

CASH WITH PERSONAL CHECKS
AND CREDIT CARDS

If you have an American Express card, you can cash personal checks at American Express offices overseas. Many foreign Automated Teller Machines (ATMs) also allow cash withdrawals upon insertion of recognized American credit cards such as American Express, Visa, and MasterCard. These companies can provide you with a list of their ATM locations overseas. There is usually a charge for cash withdrawals, sometimes up to 2 percent of the amount borrowed. American Express may require you to purchase traveler's checks in addition to cash.

At hotels which accept major credit cards, you may also be able to cash a personal check up to a specified limit, although their policies vary. However, don't count on this merely because a hotel accepts your credit card. If you are really desperate, you can have someone transfer funds to you through an American Express office or an overseas bank. To do this, the sender must go to a local American Express office and designate the foreign American Express office which is to receive the funds. Most transfers can take place overnight.

EXCHANGING MONEY AT BANKS

In most overseas countries, exchanging funds at the official rate is done at an independent money exchange (*cambio, change,* and *Wechsel* are names often used for them in other languages), at banks and at some hotels. Note that in Western countries and some Asian nations, there is no official rate but only a commercial rate, which would be more or less the same everywhere, except at hotels. There is rarely a currency black market in Western countries since the currency is freely exchangeable.

Currency exchanges will generally post signs with the prevailing exchange rate. The difference between the buy and sell rate represents the profit made by the exchanging entity, usually between 3 and 6 percent. Exchange authorities also make hidden profits by deflating their exchange rates, so if you are exchanging a large amount of money, it is best to shop around. Take a calculator with you and work out what you should be getting. You may be surprised at how often banks make mistakes.

It is a fact of life that banks always seem to be closed when you need them and open when you don't. Foreign bankers take long lunches and observe every conceivable holiday. This practice assures business for independent exchange companies and hotels, who offer poorer rates in exchange for the luxury of convenience.

If you are traveling between two foreign countries, do not exchange your local currency back into dollars before you leave and then reexchange when you arrive in the next country. This practice will result in double payment of commissions. Also, many currency exchanges refuse to accept coins, even of large denominations such as British pounds. You can, however, generally exchange coins in the country where they are issued for bank notes of another country (or the same country). Do so before you leave so you don't have to lug around sixteen pounds of *zlotys* while you are in Germany.

CREDIT CARDS

While it is true that major credit cards are accepted everywhere, this applies to countries rather than specific agencies. Within many foreign countries, plastic has limited utility. Except for Western and some Asian nations, credit cards have a much lower acceptance rate than advertisements would have you believe. Always check in advance—even with hotels—to see if they will accept your card. Restaurants are also problematic; ask which cards they take when you make reservations. Guidebooks are generally reliable for this sort of information, but restaurant policies change quickly. If you are unsure, take enough foreign currency with you to cover your meal in case an establishment has decided that paying credit card commissions is too expensive.

Using a credit card overseas has advantages and disadvantages. Credit card companies often delay overseas charges, waiting for a more favorable exchange rate (for them). While this reduces the length of time these charges are sitting in your account and accruing interest, exchange rate fluctuations can wipe out any advantage you may gain. In countries where exchange controls are present, your bill will usually be rendered at the (unfavorable) official rate.

Charges made overseas, particularly in developing countries, can also take months to clear because of simple bureaucratic snarls. Sometimes they never appear on your bill at all, although this is becoming less common as foreign merchants become more familiar with Western credit organizations.

If you use credit cards overseas, be prepared to wait awhile before the clerk returns with your voucher for signature. While some countries are connected by computer with the creditor for security checks, this is still fairly uncommon. Most clerks must cross-check cards manually against their security list of lost or stolen cards.

COVERING YOUR ACCOUNT

If you intend to be out of the country for an extended time (one month or more), make arrangements to have your credit card statement paid while you are gone. If you have exceeded your spending limit while overseas or if you are not current with payments, credit card companies may suspend your credit privileges while you are on the road. This is not only embarrassing but can sometimes be disastrous.

Making payments on your credit card can be even more difficult if you are using your personal card and the statements are delivered to your residence. You may not even see the statement until you return. This can be particularly difficult if your credit card company insists that you pay the entire outstanding amount each month.

If you are using an American Express card, you can make arrangements with them in advance to pay outstanding charges at American Express offices overseas, although many of their offices overseas cannot check your outstanding balance. If overseas payment is possible, you can do so with a personal/dollar-denominated check.

The following are some other suggestions for avoiding credit card suspension.

Use a business credit card. Business credit cards are issued by your employer and can be paid during your absence, since your employer gets the bill. Keep your receipts to reconcile your statement upon your return.

Have your personal credit card statement sent to your office. Instruct someone at the office to pay all credit card bills. If there are errors, you can correct them upon your return.

Pay in advance. Credit card companies will often carry a credit on your account while you are gone. The payment just before you leave should be substantially higher than the amount listed on your last statement.

REPLACING LOST CARDS

If you have an American Express Card, you can get an emergency replacement card at overseas American Express offices. Often, however, emergency replacement cards will not have an encoded magnetic strip on the back; you won't be able to use it in ATMs or in computerized authorization machines. You will receive an encoded replacement card at your billing address within two or three weeks. Other companies will also replace lost cards but not as quickly.

Credit card holders may also have access to an emergency assistance program. A collect phone call to your credit card company may also get you an emergency replacement card. For more information, see Other Resources.

AFFINITY CARDS

Affinity cards work like any other credit card but allow you to accumulate frequent flyer miles every time you use them. Generally you get one mile credit on your frequent flyer account for each dollar you charge to the card. Contact Visa or MasterCard for more information.

4

Packing For Your Trip

In addition to business-related items noted in the supply checklist in the beginning of this book, business travelers should pay attention to their personal travel needs. The items you will require on a business trip differ from those you would ordinarily pack for a vacation. This chapter considers the specific needs of executives traveling overseas.

LUGGAGE

As noted earlier, if you are going for a week or less, we suggest you take only carry-on luggage. Carry-on luggage is generally a garment bag and your briefcase. Your garment bag should have both a secure handle and a shoulder strap. If for some reason you are not permitted to carry on a garment bag, remove the shoulder strap and hanging hook and put them inside the bag before checking it through. Straps and hooks often get caught in the airport baggage handling equipment.

If you are traveling for more than a week, your best bet is hard-sided luggage. As noted in chapter 11, hard-sided luggage tends to deter thieves and protects your valuables better than the soft-sided variety. Luggage with built-in wheels is also a good idea. You will thank yourself after a few trips through customs.

Luggage should be selected on the basis of durability, weight, and convenience. Useful features include a built-in handle and wheels so that you don't need to rent baggage carts at the airport. Do not purchase luggage made from exotic materials such as suede. They are not durable, they are heavy, and they are needlessly expensive. In any event, impressing the baggage handlers at foreign airports is a poor idea. Expensive luggage marks you as a rich foreigner and can target you as a potential victim.

Good bets for luggage include:

- Samsonite's Piggyback (about $200, has built-in handle and wheels; a strap allows you to piggyback other bags on top of the larger case).
- Samsonite's Silhouette 4 Ultravalet garment bag (about $200, has see-through compartments as well as a packing bar that reduces wrinkles).
- American Tourister's Organizer Plus garment bag (around $200, comes with a packing checklist).

Experienced travelers, having observed the tender care given baggage by the crew who unload aircraft, put extra reinforcement around their luggage. These are nylon straps with plastic or metal retaining clips and are available at most luggage stores.

YOUR "DOP KIT"

A dop kit is really a toiletries bag. You should buy an inexpensive canvas bag with a zip closure and waterproof lining. Expensive leather bags are more likely to "grow legs" in some countries. In any event, you don't need to impress the cleaning force in foreign hotels.

In addition to your usual cosmetics or toiletries, your dop kit should contain the following (not in large quantities):

Nonprescription pharmaceuticals: Multivitamins, aspirin, cold capsules, pain-relieving lotion (Solarcaine, Absorbine Jr., etc.).

Antibiotics.

Water purification tablets: These can be bought at drugstores and outdoors/camping stores.

First-aid kit: This should contain bandages, disinfectant, sterile gauze, adhesive tape, antibiotic cream, a thermometer, antidiarrheals *(see chapter 10),* and other standard items.

Insect repellent: Both room insecticide and personal repellent.

Delousing shampoo: It is not unheard of for a business traveler to get head or body lice. This cannot only be uncomfortable but may cause serious embarrassment when you return to your spouse. Use delousing shampoo at least once a week when traveling in Third-World countries. Often, lice do not show up for two or three weeks and it is best to get rid of them before they start to itch.

Condoms: Sexual activity in many foreign countries can be fatal. Either abstain completely or take your own protection; remember, condoms are often of questionable quality. AIDS and other diseases are rampant—even if the official statistics in some countries don't acknowledge this to be the case.

Sanitary napkins/tampons: Foreign products for female hygiene are sometimes less than adequate. Take a supply with you.

Swiss army knife: You don't need to get the one with fifty-five implements, but you should at least have a knife, corkscrew, bottle opener, and tweezers. Pack it in your checked luggage if detectable as a knife *(see chapter 5,* "Security Checkpoints").

Air freshener (nonaerosol): You would be amazed at how foul some hotel rooms smell.

Extra glasses: If you lose or break your glasses (or contacts) overseas, it can be frustrating and expensive to replace them. Always take an extra pair. It is also a good idea to take your written prescription with you. In some countries, optometrists can fill it overnight. If you are going to a sunny country, don't leave your sunglasses at home. The best ones block out glare, haze, and ultraviolet light without distorting vision. Because sunglasses are considered a luxury item, buying them outside the U.S. can be expensive. Bring an extra pair so you won't incur the extra expense of replacing them. Note: in some cultures (e.g., the Middle East) wearing sunglasses in a social or business situation is not appropriate because it is considered to be deceptive to cover the eyes.

Sewing kit: These are available for less than $5 in most department stores and generally contain black, white, brown, and blue thread; needles; pins; and buttons.

Manicure scissors: Pack these in your checked luggage, not in your carry-on. If you have only carry-on bags, the implements should be very small and appear nonthreatening.

PRESCRIPTION PHARMACEUTICALS

Bring written prescriptions with you, particularly for drugs containing narcotics, both to replenish your supply and to demonstrate to foreign authorities that you are indeed required to imbibe controlled substances. The commercial and generic names of some U.S. drugs are different in foreign countries, so ask your doctor to give you a prescription which can be filled overseas. All medication should be carried in its original labeled container and packed in your carry-on luggage or briefcase. If any medications contain narcotics, carry a letter from your doctor attesting to your need to take them. Insulin users should make special arrangements in advance with their hotels to assure safe (refrigerated) storage of their ampules.

IMMERSION HEATER

An immersion heater is a small coil which can be placed in a cup to boil water. You may need to get conversion plugs for it (*see chapter 12*). Immersion heaters work on resistance and can boil a cup of water in three to five minutes. They are not only good for making coffee in the morning but can also effectively sterilize water.

ZIPLOC AND OPAQUE STORAGE BAGS

If possible, avoid taking aerosol (pressurized) cans; they frequently leak at high altitudes. If you do pack them, you can avoid a mess by sealing them in plastic bags. Opaque storage bags are also useful for concealing valuables, especially at hotels (*see chapter 7*).

CLOTHING

Don't worry about being a fashion trendsetter overseas. Take as many "mix and match" items as possible—and only a few pairs of shoes (they take up a lot of space and are heavy). As noted in chapter 2, it is wise to travel in clothing that will suffice in a business setting should your luggage be delayed or lost. Clothing should be stylish but conservative. Loud colors, unusual tailoring, and flashy accessories may not only be resented by foreigners but actually may be insulting. Women executives may prefer to take dresses and skirts rather than pants; they tend to stay cleaner and are more acceptable in many countries.

Executives who expect to attend a very formal affair overseas should carry their attire with them on the plane. Clothing costing hundreds of dollars will not be replaced by an airline if lost; the compensation limit is $500 for all luggage.

Do not take all-cotton shirts or blouses. Although they may look great the first day out, they crease easily and foreign laundries often do not know how to press them back to their original form. All shirts and blouses should have at least 40 percent synthetic content. This may not be stylish, but it is certainly practical. Do not bring wool sweaters to most overseas destinations. They are bulky, expensive, and absorb moisture; long underwear or cotton sweaters will be far easier to pack.

BLENDING IN

Unless you are very familiar with a particular country, attempts to blend in with the local population by donning indigenous garments can make you look absurd. Do not attempt to be something you are not. On informal occasions, however, it is sometimes appropriate to wear indigenous clothing. Locally made shirts and dresses, for example, can be both comfortable and attractive in informal settings. Americans should not attempt to wear local formal attire unless it is specifically requested; Westerners tend to look preposterous in Japanese kimonos.

Dress comfortably and somewhat more formally than at home. Wear the type of clothing that would be generally appropriate in a business atmosphere at home in a comparable climate. In a business environment there are certain things you should never wear (and, in some countries, should not wear under any circumstances). These include jogging shoes, T-shirts, shorts, tight-fitting sweaters (women), open-to-the-navel shirts (men), funny hats, or jeans.

SHOES

Selecting shoes can be important; they should be chosen for versatility and comfort rather than style and should be on the conservative side. If you are traveling to the Middle East or East Asia, where you will be expected to take off your shoes often (entering houses, religious edifices, etc.), slip-on shoes are a good choice, but avoid slip-ons that are too casual.

Men should take one pair of black shoes to match grey and blue suits; brown shoes should not be necessary.

If you are traveling to particularly muddy or dirty areas, you might try having an older pair of shoes resoled with neophrene about three-quarters of an inch thick. These are colloquially known as "Bucharest boots"; they keep your feet dry and are a good substitute for rubbers.

5

At the Airport/ on the Plane

YOUR TICKETS

Before reserving tickets, check to see if there are restrictions on changing your itinerary. Unless you are bound by a company rule which requires you to take the lowest-priced fare, don't do it. Low-priced fares generally have restrictions which make it difficult to change your travel plans en route.

If you purchase your ticket through a particular air carrier, some countries require you to get that airline's endorsement before you can fly on another air carrier. It is much better to purchase an "open issuance" ticket which allows you to change to another airline easily if you are overseas. Open issuance tickets are generally available only through travel agents. Tell the travel agent that you want a YY (open issuance) ticket so you can change your ticket easily overseas if necessary. Retain your ticket receipt in the event of later disputes. Keep your ticket in the ticket envelope, folded shut.

Air travel tickets are written in a format approved by the International Air Transport Association (IATA). After you have set your itinerary, look carefully at your tickets for travel dates, flight numbers, airlines, class of travel, and especially for confirmation of your reservations. Travel agents and airlines are not infallible.

CHECK-IN

First and business class generally have separate check-in counters and usually move a little faster than the economy class check-in. Arrive at least an hour before your flight time to allow for security and passport checks, customs control (in foreign countries), and mile-long lines at each of these places. But don't arrive *too* early; few airports or airlines will accept your luggage or check you in more than two hours before your departure time, and rarely that early. Long queues form quickly, however, so it can be a serious miscalculation to leave the check-in area before the desk opens only to find long lines a few minutes later.

When your ticket is returned to you, check that the only voucher which has been detached is the one for the next flight and that all remaining vouchers are still in place.

BAGGAGE

Old luggage claim tags showing a former destination are a principal cause of lost or misdirected bags and should be removed before you check any luggage.

The baggage allowance on most carriers is sixty-six pounds (thirty kilograms) for first- and business-class passengers and forty-four pounds (twenty kilograms) for everyone else. This allowance is supposed to include hand baggage, but in practice, hand baggage is rarely weighed. A wide variety of items are allowed as hand baggage, including the following:

- A small personal bag or briefcase
- An overcoat
- An umbrella or walking stick

- A small camera and pair of binoculars
- A reasonable amount of reading matter
- Collapsible wheelchairs

Many airlines overseas have given up weighing baggage and instead require it to conform to certain combined dimensions (height, plus length, plus breadth, for check-in baggage, maximum two cases). These dimensions are usually a combined maximum of sixty-two inches for regular luggage and for hand baggage a combined maximum of forty-five inches. Most airlines limit carry-on luggage to two pieces in economy class.

PREVENTING LOST LUGGAGE

Despite all your best efforts and precautions (and those of the airlines), bags get lost. The airline industry points out, however, that less than 2 percent of all bags are lost and of those lost, 95 percent are recovered and returned to their owners. You can improve your chances of having your bags awaiting you at your destination by taking a few prudent steps.

1. Have your own luggage tags which give your name and home address and telephone numbers.
2. Carry identification on the inside of your luggage in a place that will be visible when the bag is opened. One way to do this is to staple or tape your business card to the inside cover of your luggage.
3. Having a distinctive mark on the outside of each piece (in addition to your luggage tag) will help to prevent mix-ups with luggage similar in appearance. One method is to put colorful tape or decals on the side of the bag or even a piece of colored yarn no more than four inches long tied around the handle.
4. Get receipts for each bag you check and retain them until your luggage is claimed.

CHOOSING YOUR SEAT

Most airlines allow you to select a seat at the time you purchase your ticket. This need not be a random exercise on overseas flights if you give some thought to your preferences beforehand.

There is no particular advantage to having a window seat on most overseas flights; the ocean or the tundra looks pretty much the same at 30,000 feet. Aisle seats are easier to get in to and out of. On long-haul flights they also give a better view of the film, especially halfway between the cabin bulkheads. Bulkhead seats (i.e., those immediately behind a partition) have the most legroom, but sometimes they have poor viewing of the screen on movie flights. On some aircraft, however, bulkhead seats are immediately behind a television monitor and you can have both legroom *and* a good view of the screen. Seats by emergency exits also provide more legroom. Avoid middle seats if possible.

If you are traveling with a business associate, it is generally best to choose a window and an aisle seat. Airlines usually sell center seats last. If the seat between you is empty, you will have room to stretch out. If the seat is sold, one of you can always offer to exchange seats with a new passenger so you and your business associate can travel side by side. As previously noted, on undersold flights a center seat in the middle section toward the back of the plane may allow you to stretch out a bit.

Another option when traveling with a companion is to choose aisle seats across from each other in the same row. It's easier to hold a conversation with someone separated by a few feet rather than jammed in the seat next to you, despite the drawback of having to put up with occasional interruptions by passing trolleys or passengers.

Recently, airlines have taken space away from economy class to make business class sections roomier. Seat spacing (the distance between a certain point on a seat and the same point on the seat behind it), or "pitch" in airline lingo, is shrinking in economy class. In the mideighties, an economy class seat along the aisle would occupy thirty-four to thirty-six inches. Today that same seat occupies only thirty-one inches. The math behind the crunch is simple—take away one inch from each of the thirty-six economy class rows and add one row to the more profitable business class sections.

In addition to pitch, aircraft have comfort levels. The *Consumer Reports Travel Letter* believes the most comfortable planes to be the new MD-80s and the 767, the DC-10s, and the L1011s. Older 727s and 747s are in the middle range, and newer 727s, 737s, and 757s (which seat six across) are generally the least comfortable. Check with your travel agent to find out which type of aircraft you'll be flying and adjust your seat selection accordingly.

FIREARMS

Firearms generally may be transported on board, but most airlines require that (a) you declare their existence at the check-in counter, (b) the guns be separately packed in a hard-sided, locked bag, (c) they be unloaded, and (d) they be marked with tags supplied by the airline.

If you bring a firearm to the check-in counter, do not open the case. The ground personnel may ask you to go to a back room to demonstrate that the gun is indeed unloaded.

As noted in chapter 1, find out what restrictions exist in the countries you plan to pass through with regard to importation of firearms. If you are going to be stopping in a restrictive country in transit to your final destination, check the firearm all the way through to the final destination at the time of initial check-in. Attempting to pick up your gun and take it through customs in England, for example, is virtually impossible unless prior arrangements have been made. Some airlines may require you to have the ammunition packed separately from the gun. Check with your airline before departure regarding their policy.

NOTE: If you are going hunting at your final destination, ask about local regulations with regard to camouflage items. Some countries severely restrict or prohibit private individuals from wearing or even possessing camouflage gear.

INAPPROPRIATE JOKES

While you are at the airport or on any airplane, it is not only in bad taste but illegal to make jokes about bombs or hijacking. Depending upon local jurisdiction, you may be subject to arrest for even mentioning bombs.

AIRLINE CLUBS

After check-in you may want to wait for your flight in an airline club lounge. Generally much more pleasant than the main terminal, airline clubs provide telephones, reading material, televisions, and a bar. In some locations, drinks are complimentary. Airlines do not maintain airline clubs at *all* their destinations, so you may wish to go to the club of another airline if you are a member. However, clubs generally make flight announcements only for their own airline, so keep track of the time if you are flying on another carrier.

If you are flying overseas first class, you will automatically be admitted to your carrier's club, but travelers flying other classes may need a club card. There are annual fees for joining many of these clubs, or you can purchase a lifetime membership. A list of airline clubs is provided in appendix 9.

PROCEEDING TO THE GATE

Many international airports are quite large, so you should allow plenty of time to get to the gate. If you already have your boarding pass and seat assignment, you can board about fifteen minutes before departure. If you do not have a boarding pass, get to the gate at least thirty minutes before departure. Failure to check in and receive a boarding pass at least ten minutes before departure may cause the airline to assume you are a no-show and give away your seat.

SECURITY CHECKPOINTS

At check-in, you may be asked if you packed your bags yourself. This is a normal security precaution. Some airlines and airports also have rigorous screening for checked baggage, and you should assume that bags for most overseas flights will be X rayed. There are certain things which should never be packed in your baggage: explosives, corrosives (acid), ammunition, firearms, high-pressure devices, etc. If you have a question with regard to any of these, contact the airline in advance. It may be possible to have the airline transport them separately.

The most common error travelers make is carrying pocketknives or scissors in a toilet kit in their briefcases. This is strictly forbidden on most air carriers. Not only may they be confiscated, but you may have to endure close questioning by airport security and risk the chance of missing your flight. If a knife or scissors are found, you can sometimes convince the air carrier to have it separately packed and carried in the cockpit or other secure place on the aircraft. Remember that the hand-luggage security check is almost always done not by airline staff but by airport security personnel, who are less likely to be gentle and accommodating. If you do wish to carry either of these items, make sure before your flight that it is not detectable as a weapon.

At some airports you may be asked to turn on laptop computers, radios, or other electronic devices. Make sure the batteries are charged or that you have a cord with which to plug them in, to demonstrate that they are what they purport to be.

Contrary to common belief, most airport security X rays will not damage most film unless the ASA is very high (1000 or above). This is not universally true, however. If you are concerned about your film, many photography stores sell lead-foil pouches which provide absolute protection against X rays.

AT THE GATE

At certain foreign airports—particularly for short-haul flights within the same country—your boarding pass will not show a preassigned seat (i.e., there will be open seating). In these cases it is wise to be first in the queue so you can get a preferred seat.

Before actually boarding the plane, make sure you are getting on the right aircraft. Although airlines use multiple methods to ensure that passengers are on the right plane, every day someone winds up in a destination hundreds of miles away from his or her intended destination. In one well-publicized case, a passenger boarded an aircraft in San Francisco for the ten-minute trip to Oakland, California, and wound up in Auckland, New Zealand.

USING EQUIPMENT

Most airlines allow the use of standard business equipment in flight, such as dictating machines or laptop computers. You should not, however, use any radio equipment; it can cause interference with the electronics of the airplane. You can generally use your own headset for listening to the music and movie program, although in economy class the airline may charge you a rental fee for using your own headset.

EATING AND DRINKING

As most business travelers know, airline cuisine is an oxymoron. Nevertheless, it is possible to have a good meal on a plane. All major air carriers will prepare special meals on request—often at little or no charge. In addition to vegetarian and kosher dishes, airlines have a variety of other selections, and you can learn menus in advance from an airline office or by writing or calling the airline (see appendix

10). Generally, special meals require advance notice of two to three days, but exceptions may be made. These special meals generally receive more attention from the caterers and are often quite good.

Airlines strongly discourage passengers from bringing their own drinks on board—particularly alcohol. Nevertheless, it is not unusual for people to eschew the offerings of airline food and pack a brown bag for themselves for the journey.

SAFETY

Some business travelers swear that the safest seats are in the front of the plane; others believe over the wing is safest—still others prefer the tail of the plane. There is no reliable data to prove or disprove any of these theories. On the other hand, seats over the wing provide a smoother ride than those in either the forward or the rear sections, and the front of the aircraft is quieter and offers better views from the window.

Most business travelers have become immune to the safety lecture given at the beginning of every flight (or can repeat it by heart). It is important, though, to locate the emergency exits.

In the event of an emergency, the crew will give specific instructions. The most important thing to remember in an emergency is to stay in your seat and let the flight crew do their job. Do not attempt to open the emergency doors unless specifically instructed to do so.

If an emergency occurs, take off your shoes (high heels, especially, can damage the inflatable emergency slides), fasten your seat belt tightly, empty your pockets (pens can pierce your rib cage), and lean forward. After you have evacuated the aircraft, get away from the plane as quickly as possible in case of fire or explosion and also so the emergency crews can have faster access to the aircraft.

6

Arrival at Foreign Airports

IMMIGRATION AND CUSTOMS

After you leave the aircraft, the first thing you must do is clear immigration. On most overseas flights, the air crew will distribute entry forms, if the country requires them, to be filled out before you land. If you were asleep when forms were distributed, ask the flight crew for one before you leave the aircraft. Forms are available in the immigration area, but you will lose time in the queue.

In some countries the entry form is also your departure form; you will be expected to keep it with you throughout your trip. The easiest way to do this is to clip the form in your passport on the page where the visa for that country appears, or on the second page if no visa is required. Do not lose this form, as it can be a major hassle to leave the country if it is missing.

After you clear immigration, you will claim your baggage. Some airports have free baggage carts; in others you will have to pay for them. Because you thought ahead, you have luggage with built-in wheels so you should not need a cart.

The third step is customs. Some countries require that a customs declaration form be completed. Read the declaration carefully. If you have any questions, ask the customs officials upon arrival if an item needs to be declared. Do not dissemble on your customs or immigration forms; many countries have long jail terms and huge fines for smuggling.

Many foreign airports have adopted a standard international system—green and red lines—for clearing customs. Go through the green line if you have nothing to declare. If you have something to declare (or think you may have a declarable item) or if you are carrying a carnet (*see chapter 1*), go through the red line.

In all countries, guns, pharmaceuticals in excess of personal needs, currency, and valuable or luxury items such as perfume, jewelry, and even radios may be declarable. Do not guess. Customs agents in the green line randomly check passengers to catch those trying to evade the rules. The penalties in the green line are substantially higher than innocent mistakes made in the red line.

You may have to pay a *duty*, or fee, on your declarable goods. This can sometimes be a problem because duties must often be paid in local currency, and few foreign customs cashiers accept credit cards. Sometimes you will not be able to exchange currency until you have cleared customs, although you can often arrange for customs officials to let you return to the customs area after you have exchanged your money at the main airport terminal. As noted in chapter 3, if you know you will be taking declarable goods into a country, take enough local currency with you to pay the anticipated duty. Check duty rates with the foreign embassy before you leave. You should also have documents or receipts attesting to the value of declared items, or the customs officials may merely guess as to what they are worth and charge you accordingly.

Keep receipts of any customs duties you pay. If you reexport or take the product back out with you, it is sometimes possible to get a *drawback* (refund) of the duty paid, and you will need your receipt to do so. Ask the customs officials at the time you enter how you go about getting a drawback. They will generally require you to fill out forms at the time of entry specifically identifying the product. You can usually avoid this process in the case of commercial samples if you have a carnet.

LOST LUGGAGE

Even the most well-identified and registered luggage is sometimes lost. If you are sure that your bags have not arrived, immediately locate the airline representative in the baggage claim area. Lost-baggage clerks are the recipients of much abuse, so remember that a kind word can work wonders. You will be asked to fill out a lost-luggage claim form describing your luggage and indicating where it should be delivered; the delivery is generally free of charge. Be sure to tell the hotel that you are expecting your luggage so it can be brought to your room when it arrives.

If you crossed an international border on your flight, your bags cannot be delivered to you until they have cleared customs. If the bags are locked, the customs officers will generally not open them until you supply them with a key. Although sometimes you can make arrangements with a friendly lost-baggage agent to clear them for you by giving him the key, this is unusual. Further, if having strangers pawing through your luggage without supervision concerns you, you'll probably want to go back to the airport to claim it yourself anyway.

If your lost luggage contains any declarable items (valuables, guns, etc.), it will generally be kept in the customs section rather than in the airline baggage area. Check with the airline to determine where your bags will be held, and return to the airport as soon as you are notified of their arrival. Leaving luggage in foreign airports for an extended period of time is unwise.

MISSED FLIGHTS

It is not unheard-of for business travelers to miss their connections in a foreign country. If this happens, immediately seek the passenger service agent for assistance. You will generally be given a voucher for meals or even overnight accommodations by the airline on which you arrived. Your voucher may have a stub to be torn off by the receptionist/cashier at the hotel and given to you; keep this with the rest of your receipts. If you do not have a visa for the country in which you are stranded, the passenger service agent will assist you in getting a temporary transit visa. Sometimes the airline will have a transit hotel at the airport itself, particularly in Europe.

7

At the Hotel

CHECKING IN

When you arrive at the hotel, you may be met by a person who offers to take your bags. If you can carry your own bags in, do so. Often, the "porters" outside a hotel are not hotel employees but locals looking to make a few bucks from tourists. Retrieving your bag from these people is sometimes an effort, even with a large bribe. If you have too many bags to carry yourself, follow the porter into the hotel—do not leave him with your bags on the sidewalk.

Have your written hotel confirmation with you when you check in. It is a source of constant amazement to business travelers how easily foreign hotels can lose confirmed reservations. Many foreign hotels do not have facsimile machines, so you should be able to present a telex confirmation either from your travel agent or from the hotel itself. This is very important, as the person confirming reservations may never have checked with the front desk and your room may have consequently been given away. If you have written confirmation, you can usually persuade the clerk (or the manager) to give you the room you had originally booked.

Unlike most American hotels, foreign hotels sometimes fail to ask for an impression of your credit card. They may instead ask to see or keep your passport. If this occurs, politely inquire how long it will be retained; it should not be for more than a few hours. One way to avoid separation from your passport is to travel with photocopies of the first two pages, as suggested in chapter 1. These pages include all the information the hotel will need as well as your picture. If the hotel will not accept a photocopy but insists upon retaining your passport, ask for it constantly until it is returned. In unstable countries, you should not leave the hotel without your passport.

Sometimes the desk clerk will assign a porter to carry your bags for you; other times, you will be expected to carry them yourself. Before dismissing the porter, make sure the lights, television, and air conditioning work; the toilet flushes; the door locks; and water flows from the taps. If not, request to be moved to another room. Most foreign hotels—even in developing countries—actually have higher-quality rooms available for special people; you want to be one of them.

Tipping is generally not only acceptable but expected in some circumstances. Tipping practices vary widely; refer to country-specific tourist guidebooks for tipping guidelines.

FIRE SAFETY

Pay careful attention to exits. Fire codes in many foreign countries are lacking in specificity, and it is important to know how to get out if necessary. Read the fire safety instructions in your room, and make sure you understand how to report a fire. Count the doors between your room and the nearest exit—this could be a lifesaver if you have to crawl through a smoke-filled corridor.

SECURITY

When unpacking, leave anything that is reasonably valuable locked in your suitcase or in the hotel safe. Put your valuable items (jewelry, money, traveler's checks, etc.) in the opaque plastic bag you brought with you and take it to the front desk. Ask for access to the safe.

Generally, the clerk will give you a key and lead you to the safe, which will usually contain safe-deposit boxes operating on a dual-key system. The clerk's key must be inserted first in order for yours to open the box. Wait until the clerk leaves before putting your valuables in the safe; if he or she does not, at least your valuables are discreetly concealed in the opaque bag. You will be asked to sign a card indicating your room number, and sometimes your time of entry and exit will be requested as well.

Ordinarily, use of a hotel safe is free of charge, although there may be a nominal fee for bulky items. Never put your passport in the safe; carry it with you at all times. You may, however, want to put proof of citizenship (such as a copy of your birth certificate or your passport photocopies) in the safe in case your passport is lost or stolen. This will help you get a temporary passport more quickly from the local American embassy but it is not legally required.

YOUR ROOM

In many countries, even Western ones, hotel rooms used by foreign business executives are bugged. This should not ordinarily be a cause of great consternation, but you should be aware that it may be a part of overseas travel. One Western business executive commented that the Swiss have the most discreet—but efficient—security service in the world. They know what everyone is doing twenty-four hours a day. They would never embarrass you—but they know. Other security services are not nearly as discreet.

Do not attempt to defeat bugging devices in your hotel room. Loud music and running water only attract further attention from local security services; they will redouble their efforts, thinking you have something to hide. It is best to simply not do or say anything in your room which might compromise you or your company.

MEALS

In many hotels outside the United States, breakfast is automatically included in your room charge, but you may wish to confirm this at the front desk. The hours for breakfast will often be listed on a board somewhere near the reception desk or with the information you receive when you check in. When you go to breakfast, be sure to bring your room key with you and place it face up on the table. The staff will often merely take note of the charge, and you will not even receive a bill or check to sign. When included in the room charge, breakfast, with the exception of beverages, is generally buffet-style.

8

Eating, Drinking, and Entertaining Abroad

Foreign business executives are often invited to social events during the course of their overseas travels. These events are often less social occasions than business rituals. While customs in countries vary, the following guidelines apply almost anywhere (see the Bibliography for suggested resources).

INVITATIONS

If you are traveling with a group and are invited to a meal, to an entertainment event, or to someone's home, make sure that you understand the scope of the invitation. Does it include just you, or are your colleagues invited as well? If you are traveling with your family, does it include them? There are no firm rules as to how to obtain this information; strategies vary from country to country. Consult sources

51

cited in the Bibliography and, if you have an interpreter or local colleague, make discreet inquiries as to who is expected to appear at a function. Make no assumptions about the nature of the invitation. It is just as embarrassing to show up alone when the host is expecting the entire delegation as to do the opposite.

PUNCTUALITY

In some countries, such as in northern Europe, punctuality is not only courteous but obligatory. There is no such thing as being "fashionably late" in Frankfort, even for a social engagement. In other cultures, showing up on time in someone's home may catch the host still in the shower with the canapés yet unmade.

It is very important to observe local custom in this regard. Consult guidebooks, your colleagues, and even your hotel concierge before assuming that promptness is welcome. There are, of course, exceptions to local custom in every country. Military types tend to be sticklers for punctuality in every clime, and rock concerts rarely begin promptly anywhere.

MEALS

American businesspeople will often be treated to local delicacies at meals. These are usually painstakingly prepared and are regarded as a particular honor. Whether you feel honored or not when confronted with camel meat simmered in yogurt or sea cucumbers (slugs) in a delicate sauce, you must at least try some. A small helping is generally adequate; slicing a very thin piece of whatever you are offered so that it can be swallowed in one gulp is also a useful skill to master.

Be sensitive to local table manners and try to take cues from your hosts. In Middle Eastern countries, for example, it is impolite to eat with your left hand. In Japan, one never leaves one's chopsticks sticking up from the rice. Leaving a lot of food on one's plate is acceptable in Europe but not in Southeast Asia. Belching after a meal is popular in Bulgaria, but as your mother told you, not in Western

countries. Again, consult country-specific books on etiquette to avoid making a fool of yourself.

DRINKING

In many foreign cultures, the ability to consume immense amounts of alcoholic beverages is regarded as necessary for good business relationships. Even if you have the constitution of a tank and the liver of a woolly mammoth, do not attempt to keep up with your hosts. No matter how effete they may seem, white wine spritzers do have their place. Beer is sometimes an adequate substitute for the local punch, as it can fill you up before you get too drunk. Other ploys include feeding the potted palms and drinking great quantities of water, which gives you an excuse to go to the rest room at frequent intervals (this also helps with dehydration the next day).

TIPPING

Before you pay for meals or drinks, be sure to check to see whether a service charge has been included in the bill. Double tipping, while appreciated, is likely to mark you as a boob.

CAROUSING

After-hours carousing is usually (though not exclusively) limited to men. You should monitor your behavior particularly carefully in these circumstances; loose libidos are even more dangerous than loose lips. Remember, these are business contacts, with different standards from your own. Furthermore, tales of your exploits will get about quickly and may even make it back home before you do. In state-controlled countries, moreover, your carousing partners are almost certainly part of the state *apparat* and you can be sure your activities will find their way into a dossier in the secret police head-quarters. *This is not an exaggeration.*

Despite all of the above admonitions, it is still possible to have a good time at social functions with your foreign business partners. Eating exotic foods, drinking unpronounceable beverages, and seeing your hosts in their own milieu is memorable.

9

About Language

One of the biggest barriers most business travelers must overcome when visiting a foreign country is language. There are several different approaches to this problem.

FEIGNING IGNORANCE

One experienced international negotiator for a major American corporation speaks four languages passably. When he is in a country in which one of these languages is the mother tongue, he pretends he understands none of what is being spoken. He believes this gives him an advantage; he can understand conversations which are meant to be private and can sometimes gain useful information.

This tactic has a myriad of pitfalls. If the foreign parties suspect you *do* speak their language, it is easy for them to lay false trails. It is also more than a little impolite to refuse to utter the simplest phrases (such as "please," and "thank you,") in a local language. In most cases, perfidy will out, and your feigned ignorance will be discovered, thereby substantially reducing your credibility in the eyes of everyone concerned.

FEIGNING EXPERTISE

Feigned expertise is just as dangerous as feigned ignorance. Some individuals master a few phrases in the local language and can say them with only a slight American accent: "Good morning, I'm Timothy Jones. You're looking fine this bright day." Your hosts will often take relatively fluent greetings (particularly if they are spoken rapidly) to imply that you are fully conversant in their tongue and will expect you to grasp all the nuances of rapid-fire conversation. This can be disastrous. It is almost as hard to deny that you speak a language once you've demonstrated your ability in it as it is to pretend that you don't speak one at all.

HIGH SCHOOL REDUX

The high school redux tactic is to exhibit no more and no less knowledge of the local language than you actually possess. The best way to do this is to plunge straight in, grammatical errors and all. It will soon become apparent to your foreign hosts whether your language is good enough for social purposes; and if they speak better English than you do their language, they will probably switch to the former. If they do not, and you are unsure of what is being said to you, ask them in English to repeat themselves.

It is always better to conduct negotiations in your mother tongue. Even if you are fluent in another language, switch to English at every opportunity. It not only gives you a negotiating advantage, but it enables you to be sure that you at least understand everything *you* say.

INTERPRETERS

Interpreters will often be provided at business meetings. They can be very helpful, if utilized properly, and an impediment if they are not.

Interpreters generally use a technique called *concurrent translation* in large meetings where the participants have headphones. The interpreter is often in a soundproof room, watching and listening to the discussion. He or she translates what is said almost as rapidly as it is spoken. Concurrent translation greatly speeds up negotiations and allows a free flow of ideas. Because of the vagaries of various languages, however, precise meanings are sometimes muddled. A German speaker, for example, may expound for what seems like forever before even coming to a verb, and the entire context of a sentence may change by inserting a triple negative at the end. When the interpretation is concurrent, pause after each twenty-five words or so to allow the translator to convey the message.

Sequential translation is more common in smaller meetings. The speaker pauses after each sentence or so to allow the interpreter to translate. This almost doubles the negotiating time and creates a rather stilted atmosphere. Nevertheless, sequential translation often delivers a more accurate sense of the intent of the speakers and allows them time to carefully phrase their next comment.

When using an interpreter it is important to speak slowly and distinctly. Always look at and speak to the person you are addressing, not the interpreter. Although a good interpreter is unobtrusive and makes the job look easy, it is a very psychologically stressful occupation. Interpreters are not machines, and compliments and fairly frequent breaks are appreciated. See the article by Jan Berris in the Bibliography for more information on interpreters.

AMERICAN ENGLISH:
NOT THE UNIVERSAL LANGUAGE

When you speak American English, it is possible—indeed, probable— that you will be misunderstood if you inject Americanisms into your language. Jargon, humor, special vocabulary, and odd grammatical structures can cause serious misunderstandings among foreigners. Americans are fond of idiomatic speech, and we sometimes do not appreciate that foreigners take literally the terms we use. The American negotiator who has "kicked back" may be assumed to be flat on his posterior. Americans are also fond of sports analogies, but few Saudis appreciate or even understand allusions to being "thrown a

curveball," "having three strikes against you," or "punting when in doubt." Buzzwords are even more fatal in discussions with foreigners. "State-of-the-art," "relevant," and "buzzword" should be excised from your lexicon when dealing with foreign business associates.

A partial list of words and phrases commonly used in American business negotiations which should not be used outside of their literal context follows. Remember that these are only examples; new phrases are born every Tuesday, and experienced business executives should be able to recognize and avoid business jargon when overseas.

abort (when meaning stop)	above the line
bottom line	caring
common ground	consciousness
downtime	dynamite
feedback	feelings
flow	gridlock
heavy hitter	in touch with
kicked back	laid back
LBO	level playing field
overview	power lunch
parameters	red ink
relate to	relevant
sandbag	TKO

RELIGIOUS ALLUSIONS

While few businesspeople ever intend to deliberately insult another religion, they sometimes do so unknowingly. A "Thank God" spoken innocently in Islamic countries can be easily misinterpreted. Similarly, common phrases such as "Jesus Christ" or "God damn it" can warrant expulsion from certain countries (Saudi Arabia, for example).

NEGOTIATING

When you are conducting international negotiations, be particularly careful to be clear and concise. Even when you use your best grammar, avoid jargon, and speak slowly, it is still possible to be misinterpreted. Negotiators with strong regional accents will need to monitor their language especially carefully. One of the best ways to illustrate your meaning during negotiations is to use as many visual materials as possible; utilizing written materials and graphics are both effective strategies. You should always follow up your negotiating sessions with written confirmation of what was negotiated or resolved. This is particularly important when using numbers. Other languages, particularly French and German, have ways of expressing numbers verbally which can be misinterpreted. During the course of negotiations *write down* any numbers that you are discussing and confirm them later with your counterpart.

There are many negotiating styles, and no single method will work equally well everywhere. The "I'm OK—You're OK" approach may work well in Sweden but be regarded as effete in Georgia (the country). Alternatively, intimidation techniques can score points in New York, but you will lose respect in Tokyo with a confrontational style. The more familiar you are with a country's history, culture, and business and social etiquette, the more effectively you can adjust your negotiating strategy. Several excellent books on international negotiation are listed in the Bibliography.

GESTURES

People around the world use body movements, or gestures, to convey specific messages. Though members of different cultures sometimes use the same gestures, they often have different meanings. Misunderstandings over gestures occur frequently in cross-cultural communication, and their misinterpretation can lead to business complications and social embarrassment. For example, the "OK" sign commonly used in the United States has several different meanings depending on the country. In France, it means "zero"; in Japan, it is a symbol for money; and in Brazil, it carries a vulgar connotation.

Americans should always avoid backslapping or touching a foreigner unless such behavior is initiated by the foreigner. Female executives should be particularly sensitive to initiating physical contact with foreigners. In some countries, even something as rudimentary as a handshake by a woman can be misinterpreted.

Your posture, stance, or distance from a foreigner can also convey unintended messages. For example, putting your feet up with the soles exposed to an Arab or Southeast Asian is insulting, and taking off your coat without an invitation in a Japanese negotiating session confirms you as a rube. Watch your hosts and follow their example.

10

Staying Healthy

No matter what your destination is, traveling abroad poses risks to your health. Although travelers may attempt to stay as healthy as possible, even the most health- and fitness-conscious business executives often have a difficult time keeping up their exercise programs and avoiding illness while overseas. This chapter will explain some easy ways to stay in shape and to avoid health problems while on the road.

KEEPING FIT

Water-Fillable Hand Weights

Lightweight, polymer hand weights can be filled with tap water to produce five- or ten-pound weights (available from Ideal Gift Company, 149-04 Veterans Memorial Highway, Suite 105, Kommack, NY 11725; tel. (800) 999-3919).

Jogging

Jogging is an excellent way to stay fit overseas, but you must be sensitive to local customs. Women in particular should be aware that certain countries disapprove of a woman disrobed to the point where she would feel comfortable jogging, particularly in Africa and the Middle East.

Jogging can also be hazardous in unfamiliar areas. Rough parts of town sometimes exist cheek by jowl with the toniest districts. Stay in areas that are reasonably safe; your hotel concierge can often recommend appropriate routes.

Swimming

Swimming is great exercise, but you should use reasonable caution overseas. Foreign swimming pools are not always entirely antiseptic. A once-a-month cleaning is the norm in some locations and may be done even less frequently in others. If you are staying in a major American-owned hotel overseas, the same standards will generally apply as those in the United States. If you are in an out-of-the-way place, it might be best to avoid the pool in favor of other forms of exercise.

Ankle Weights

Some travelers prefer to exercise during all waking hours by wearing such things as ankle weights. These are sand- or lead-filled pouches which strap around your ankles. They weigh two to five pounds, can be worn under trousers, and greatly increase the effort it takes to walk. Note that ankle weights filled with lead may set off security devices at airports.

HEALTH CONCERNS

IAMAT

The International Association for Medical Assistance to Travelers (IAMAT) has developed a network of centers throughout most of the world. The organization offers a membership packet which includes a directory of IAMAT centers with addresses and phone numbers, an immunization chart, a personal medical record folder, and a membership card. This packet takes about six weeks to arrive and is free of charge, but IAMAT is largely supported by donations; most subscribers send one with their request. Thus, when you are traveling and need a doctor or emergency help, you have a number to call for a list of approved doctors, both general practitioners and specialists, who are on duty for that particular twenty-four-hour period, including Sundays and holidays. These physicians are selected according to a review of their professional qualifications, their ability to speak English, and their acceptance of a fixed-fee schedule. For information contact IAMAT at 736 Center Street, Lewiston, NY 14092; tel. (716) 754-4883. Additional lists of English-speaking doctors can be obtained by contacting Intermedic, 777 Third Avenue, New York, NY 10017; tel. (212) 486-8974.

Allergies

If you are allergic to any medication, write down (or have someone else write down) all such allergies on a piece of paper *in the language of the country you are visiting* and paperclip it in your passport on the page where your picture appears. The following is a sample format:

ATTENTION: THE BEARER IS ALLERGIC TO PENICILLIN. In the event of an emergency do not administer anything containing this drug. A full medical history of the bearer can be obtained from Dr. B. Sawbones, 434 Maple Street, Fairfax, VA, U.S.A.; tel. (703) 123-4567.

Also make a notation concerning allergies or other medical problems in your ICV, and bring it with you when you check into any foreign medical facility. Notations in your ICV are, of course, in English.

Immunization

As noted in chapter 1, AIDS clearance and immunizations may be required, or at least desirable, before you travel to a foreign country, particularly the tropics. Consult the embassy of each country you plan to visit for their requirements, then contact your local physician; he or she will often refer you to a specialty immunization clinic for travelers. These clinics are located in major U.S. cities and have up-to-date information concerning immunization, including updates on cholera, meningitis, malaria, and typhoid as well as booster shots as necessary. Most specialty clinics also have the ICV booklet available (*see chapter 1*), and you can fill it out on the spot.

Some countries give "shots on the spot" for travelers without proof of inoculation—that is, they may insist upon administering these inoculations at the airport for a fee before you are cleared to enter the country. Although it may require some negotiation, do not accept the proffered immunization; if necessary, pay the fee and refuse the shot. In some countries, health standards are such that there is more chance of acquiring an ailment from inoculations than there is of disease prevention.

A helpful guide to immunizations and preventive measures for international travel is the inexpensive booklet, *Health Information for International Travel*. It is available from the Superintendent of Documents, U.S. Government Printing Office, Washington, DC 20402. The U.S. Public Health Services Quarantine Division also has immunization recommendations (tel. (404) 639-2572). See the Other Resources for additional health-related publications.

AIDS Testing

Many countries require long-term residents and students to submit proof that they are free from the HIV virus. Inquire at the embassies of the countries to which you are traveling whether an AIDS test is required and if certified test results from the United States are accepted. If not, find out the nature of the test and if it is permissible to supply your own disposable needle.

Diseases to Watch Out for

According to a British consumer magazine, the percentage of travelers who become ill abroad varies considerably from country to country. Several areas seem to cause a higher incidence of discomfort in foreign visitors than others, particularly stomach upset and heat, motion, and altitude sickness. Among these countries and areas are Egypt, Turkey, Latin America, Thailand, and the West Indies. These problems can be avoided or minimized by observing the food and water precautions listed under "Traveler's Diarrhea" and taking some simple, commonsense measures, such as wearing sunscreen, not overdoing athletics in an unfamiliar climate, and making sure to get enough sleep.

There are, however, some more serious afflictions to be guarded against. Diseases exist overseas which appear only in medical textbooks at home. You can avoid becoming a specimen for your local medical faculty, however, by observing the following advice.

Cholera. Given the recent outbreaks of cholera, especially in Latin America, be sure to inquire about its incidence in the countries to which you are traveling and get an inoculation if one is required (or even just recommended).

Malaria. A new antimalarial drug called *Mefloquine,* labeled *Lariam* in stores, has been shown to be effective against malaria parasites that have developed a resistance to earlier antimalarial drugs. Dosage is generally determined by the length of stay in the area and is prescribed by a physician.

Typhoid. An oral vaccine against typhoid fever called *Ty21a,* available in Europe for some time, has now been licensed for use in the United States. Previously, typhoid vaccine in this country was administered by injection. Because of the oral vaccine's comparative efficiency and minimal side effects, it should be the vaccine of choice for travelers journeying to areas where the disease is prevalent— particularly Africa, Asia, and Central and South America.

As some vaccines and drugs should not be taken simultaneously and some need to be administered well ahead of departure, make sure you inform your doctor of your itinerary early so that you may plan an appropriate schedule of inoculations, vaccines, and drugs.

Traveler's Diarrhea

Between 20 and 50 percent of travelers heading for areas considered at high risk for diarrhea can expect to be hampered by the illness. These areas include but are not limited to Latin and Central America, Africa, Asia, and the Middle East. To protect yourself when visiting these areas, observe some standard dietary precautions.

- Don't drink tap water or use it to brush your teeth. Use bottled water for teeth, and limit yourself to carbonated sodas and juices, beer, wine, and beverages made from boiled water, such as tea and coffee.

- Avoid green salads and other raw vegetables that may have been washed with contaminated water.
- Eat only fruit that you peel yourself with clean hands.
- Make sure meat, fish, and poultry have been well cooked.
- Avoid milk and other dairy products, including ice cream sold by street vendors and milk or cream in coffee or tea.
- Don't take ice in your drinks unless you know it was made from purified water.
- Skip the hotel's buffet lunch that may have sat under the sun for hours.

Business travelers may also consider taking Pepto-Bismol tablets as a preventive to traveler's diarrhea. Taking two tablets at a time, four times daily for up to three weeks can be a safe and effective means of reducing its occurrence.*

Should you come down with diarrhea despite your best efforts, try Pepto-Bismol in liquid form (rather than tablets) or Imodium A-D, a caplet sold over the counter in drugstores or pharmacies. These caplets contain an antimotilty agent that relieves the symptoms of diarrhea by slowing the intestinal movement.

If diarrhea persists or worsens, consult a physician. The doctor may prescribe antibiotics, such as Bactrim. Bactrim can stop the symptoms of diarrhea in as little as an hour when used with one of the over-the-counter antidiarrheals such as Imodium A-D. Used alone, Bactrim can shorten the course of traveler's diarrhea from a typical three- to five-day attack to one lasting only a day or a day and a half. Business travelers may want to consult their physician about obtaining a supply of Bactrim or other antibiotics before departure.

Other nonmedicinal steps can help you get through a bout with diarrhea more comfortably. To combat the dehydration which tends to accompany diarrhea, drink canned fruit juices and caffeine-free soft drinks and eat salted crackers. Orange juice, tomato juice, and bananas help maintain potassium levels. Avoid milk and other dairy products.

---

* If you opt to take any of the over-the-counter medications recommended in this chapter, be sure to follow all conditions and instructions listed on the package. If these are written in a foreign language, have them translated before taking the medication.

A useful publication on this topic is *How To Avoid Traveler's Diarrhea*, published by IAMAT.

OBTAINING MEDICAL ATTENTION

It is bad enough to be sick or injured at home, but when you are in a foreign country, getting medical attention can be daunting, particularly if you don't understand the language. By definition, you will not be at your best and sometimes cannot afford to wait. The following points should be adhered to in the case of serious illness or injury.

Contact the closest embassy or consulate: One of the main responsibilities of consular personnel is to assist their citizens who are in trouble. U.S. consulates overseas can be reached twenty-four hours a day and can recommend doctors or hospitals. A list of U.S. embassies with consular offices can be found in appendix 3.

Consult hotel personnel: Most foreign hotels which cater to foreign business executives have lists of medical personnel who speak English. Ask the desk to contact such individuals.

Utilize your IAMAT membership: As noted on page 63, IAMAT membership will provide you with a number to contact in an emergency for recommended doctors on call in your area.

Don't worry about insurance: Unlike American hospitals, most foreign hospitals do not require you to fill out insurance forms in quadruplicate before restarting your heart. Further, many American insurance policies cover medical treatment abroad, but you will have to file the claim yourself; a foreign hospital rarely will do so. Get treatment first, worry about costs later. Be sure, however, to get a detailed bill when you leave the hospital so that you can file your insurance claims when you get home. You should ascertain your medical coverage before you leave. Note that Medicare programs do not provide payment for hospitals or medical services outside of the United States.

Get only the minimum treatment: Medical care overseas is sometimes not up to the standards you might expect at home. If possible, have the minimum treatment necessary which will enable you to return home safely, and check with your local physician for follow-up examination and treatment upon your return to the U.S.

Take an active role in your hospital treatment: Hospital care in Third-World countries can be problematic. In some countries, local hospitals can be so crowded that your condition can worsen just as a result of your extended wait for medical attention. Most large cities have several hospitals. If possible, find out which one has the best reputation before you travel, and try to familiarize yourself with it upon arrival in case you need emergency medical care during your stay.

Once you are admitted, take an active role in trying to understand what doctors and nurses are doing. Ask questions, but be aware that in some countries it is not common practice to inform patients about their illness or discuss it with them. If the hospital personnel do not speak English, a phrase book can be helpful. Ask for an interpreter, even if it is the bilingual patient in the next bed. As noted in chapter 9, avoid communicating with gestures alone as they can be misinterpreted.

11

Staying Out of Trouble

TRAVELING IN TROUBLED AREAS

Business executives are often required to travel to areas where there is civil strife. While such journeys are not recommended, they are sometimes necessary, and the trip can be made easier and safer if the following rules are observed.

Check with the State Department and with the embassy. U.S. embassies and consulates overseas constantly monitor the political situations in their areas of jurisdiction and report to the State Department. Based on these reports, the State Department issues advisories for U.S. citizens traveling abroad through its citizens' emergency center in the U.S. (tel. (202) 647-5225). Sometimes these advisories urge Americans to avoid certain parts of the country because of terrorism, political turmoil, or violent crime. Often, the consular officers in-country will follow up to make sure you have been taken care of. Once you are in-country, check with the American Citizens Service Unit at the U.S. embassy or consulate for the most recent information before proceeding to a high-tension area. Remember, however, that the embassies and consulates are not travel agencies. If you are in serious trouble, they will help, but don't abuse the privilege. A list of U.S. embassies with consular offices can be found in appendix 3.

While you are at the embassy or consulate, be sure to register so that you can be reached if necessary. Give them a copy of your itinerary and a list of people to contact in the event of an emergency. This will also make it easier for you to be contacted in case of an emergency at home. In accordance with the Privacy Act, information on your welfare or whereabouts may not be released to inquirers without your authorization.

When you register with the embassy, bring your U.S. passport with you. Your passport data will be recorded, thereby simplifying the process of applying for a replacement passport should it be lost or stolen. (After you return from a troubled area, check in with the embassy to assure them that you are still vertical.)

Do not carry firearms into areas of political unrest. In times of civil strife, the best protection you may have is your neutral status. If people with guns are unsure of your loyalties, carrying a weapon can only further jeopardize your safety.

Be cautious about what you discuss with strangers. It is inadvisable to tell strangers (or speak where you can be overhead by eavesdroppers) anything about your plans or itinerary. It is also a good idea to keep your political and religious opinions to yourself. What you may regard as a nonthreatening show of interest and curiosity about your host country may be easily misinterpreted. Gathering facts can be dangerous.

Avoid luggage tags, clothing, and behavior which can identify you as an American. Too bad, but some folks don't like Yanks. If identification is included on the inside of your bags, outside identification may not be necessary while you are not in transit.

Avoid obvious terrorist targets such as bars and restaurants where Westerners tend to congregate. This is the most difficult advice to follow, but wise nevertheless.

Leave your camera in your suitcase. Warring factions rarely like to pose for photographs and can get downright nasty if they perceive you as anything other than a business executive. If you must take pictures, be sure that they are of inoffensive subjects. Taking pictures of military installations; broadcasting facilities; or the interiors of religious buildings, factories, and even libraries and bridges can be prohibited in many countries. Never take pictures of military or police personnel who are obviously guarding some government facility.

Take a first-aid kit. In areas of civil strife or where natural disasters such as floods or earthquakes occur frequently, you may need to repair minor injuries yourself. Medical personnel may be unavailable or otherwise occupied with more serious cases.

Keep your passport with you at all times. It is not unusual in troubled areas for authorities to repeatedly request identification. If you lose your passport overseas, report the loss or theft to the local police and the nearest U.S. embassy or consulate. A new passport can usually be issued within twenty-four hours; as previously noted, this process will be facilitated by making photocopies and registering with the embassy. If you discover your passport is missing while in the United States, immediately call the State Department Passport Services at (202) 647-0518, or the nearest passport agency. An agency employee will register the passport lost and make arrangements to issue a new one, usually within two weeks.

Leave no personal or business papers in your hotel room.

Watch for people following you or loiterers observing your comings and goings.

Keep a mental note of safe havens such as police stations, hotels, and hospitals.

Avoid predictable times and routes of travel.

Refuse unidentified packages.

Do not argue with bearded men carrying assault rifles. "Yes, Sir" is the appropriate response to almost any request made by such individuals.

Stay away from "hot spots." In any case of natural disaster or civil strife, some areas will be more severely affected than others. Bullets and falling buildings are not discriminating in their targets. Try to be as inconspicuous as possible, and do not let your curiosity get the best of you; do not seek a front-row seat to a revolution or typhoon.

Select guides carefully. Be extremely cautious when considering hiring a guide. If the reason for the unrest is a natural disaster, a guide can be useful in interpreting your desires. But if the situation is one of civil unrest, having a guide from "the wrong side" can be more trouble than it is worth. During rebellions, people are understandably nervous about espionage and *agents provocateurs*. In these circumstances you may be better off with a guidebook and foreign language phrase book than a flesh-and-blood guide. *Advise your family and company of your general itinerary and expected date of return.* Also give them a time that they should expect a call from you to confirm your safety. You—and they—should understand that telephone communication in troubled areas is often disrupted, and it is sometimes impossible to complete the telephone call at the appointed time. The time for company or family to get nervous should not be the date of your expected return, but two or three days later. Nevertheless, make every effort to contact appropriate people as soon as possible after you have left the disturbed region.

If in doubt, get out. There are very few business pursuits that are literally worth your life. If things are more dangerous than you presumed, get out while you can. In the past three decades, hundreds of Americans have been trapped in unpleasant situations for weeks which they could have walked away from had they left twelve hours earlier.

PERSONAL SECURITY AND THEFT

When traveling overseas, use the same precautions against violence and theft that you would at home. Women executives should be particularly careful. Some countries, particularly in the Middle East, will hold a woman responsible for any assault that may befall her if she dresses provocatively. (However unfair this may seem, it is a fact of life which is only slowly changing in many parts of the world.)

There are a number of specific precautions which can reduce your chances of becoming a victim of violence or theft.

1. Keep a low profile, and refrain from loud conversations, arguments, or conspicuous behavior which might attract attention. Dress and behave conservatively, avoiding flashy clothes, jewelry, luggage, or rented cars. Do not take unnecessary jewelry on business trips abroad. Consider purchasing an inexpensive watch, and leave the Rolex at home.

2. Make a note of emergency telephone numbers you may need: police, fire, your hotel, nearest U.S. embassy or consulate. Know how to use a pay phone and have proper change or tokens on hand.

3. Get a claim check for each piece of luggage you check at the airport, and never leave your luggage unattended in *any* public place.

4. Travel with hard-sided luggage which can be locked. Locks on most luggage will not deter an experienced thief, but can reduce petty pilferage. Leave your more valuable belongings in your suitcase, and lock it when you leave your hotel room. If you *are* robbed, file a report with the local police, and keep a copy of the police report for submission to your insurance company when you return home. In any event, make a list of all the items you are missing. To the extent that they are not covered by insurance, you may be able to take a casualty loss on your taxes.

5. Book a room between the second and seventh floors (prevents easy entrance from the outside yet is low enough for fire equipment to reach).

6. Avoid dangerous areas. Don't use shortcuts, narrow alleys, or poorly lit streets. Try not to travel alone at night. If

mugged, cooperate with the assailants; do not frighten them or fight back. In some foreign countries, a foreigner fighting with a local results in sympathetic onlookers siding with the miscreant rather than the victim.

7. When you leave your hotel, make sure to inform someone of when you plan to return.

8. Always wear a money belt. Money belts come in various shapes. One of the best is a simple leather wallet with a zipclosure about four inches by six inches and a loop at one end. Men should pass their belt through the loop and tuck the wallet inside their trousers. Women should wear this under their garments in a place where it is modestly accessible, but completely covered. Other money belts wrap around your waist under your shirt or blouse. Your money belt should contain at least enough hard currency to get you home, one credit card, and your passport. Wear your money belt at all times during waking hours. At night it is sometimes best to lock the money belt and its contents in a hotel safe. It is not unheard of for burglars to enter your room while you are asleep.

9. Always leave your plane tickets, jewelry, and other valuables locked in the hotel safe until you need them.

10. Do not use the "Please Clean My Room" sign provided by the hotel. This merely advertises your absence. Keep your room locked at all times, and never give your room number to people you don't know well. Meet any visitors in the lobby.

11. Women should carry handbags in a secure manner to prevent snatch-and-run thievery. Bags with strong shoulder straps are recommended. Men should keep their wallets in buttoned pockets, preferably inside their jackets. To guard against thieves on motorcycles, walk on the inside of sidewalks and carry your purse on the side away from the street.

VEHICLE SECURITY

If you plan to drive while overseas, familiarize yourself with local driving rules and the meaning of local road signs before you get behind the wheel. Some of this information is available from the American Automobile Association, but you should also check with the local automobile club or, in the case of rental cars, from the rental car agency.

There are several security measures which should be observed.

- Drive the more common kinds of locally available cars; even if there are American cars available, don't insist on an American model.
- Make sure the car is in good repair.
- Keep car doors locked at all times.
- Wear seat belts.
- If possible, try to avoid traveling at night.
- Don't park your car on the street overnight if the hotel has a garage or secure area. If you must park it on the street, select a well-lit area.
- If you are stopped at a roadblock, be courteous and responsive to questions asked by persons in authority. At night, turn on the interior light of the car so you can be easily and quickly identified.
- Don't leave valuables in the car.
- Never pick up hitchhikers.
- Don't get out of the car if there are suspicious individuals nearby. Drive away.
- If your car appears to have been tampered with, do not touch it. Report your suspicions to the authorities immediately.

TROUBLE WITH THE AUTHORITIES

Foreigners unaccustomed to local laws sometimes get in trouble with the local constabularies. This can be as mundane as a speeding ticket or as serious as being accused of espionage. Still, most trouble with police overseas arises from the same kinds of actions which would be illegal at home.

Conflict can often be avoided by prudent and cautious behavior. Do not do anything in a foreign country that would be legally questionable at home. Some countries have severe penalties for what would be minor infractions at home. Mere possession of pornography or minute amounts of marijuana in some countries is punishable by lengthy jail terms. The same is true in certain Islamic countries for possession or consumption of alcohol. If in doubt, consult the embassy of the foreign country before you leave home. Tourist guidebooks can also provide useful information regarding local laws and what happens if you are arrested.

It is wise to assume you have few rights. Few countries have adopted the full panoply of legal protections for the accused that the United States has. Foreign police often do not have a finely honed sense of due process. While you are in a foreign land, you are subject to their laws and procedures. If you are arrested, however, you do have the right to speak with the American consular authorities. *You should insist on this.* Be calm, but state firmly that you will cooperate with the police only after you have had an opportunity to speak with the American consulate. You will often be told that this will prolong your incarceration. This is sometimes true in that it may take a day or two before the American consular officer can see you. Nevertheless, total cooperation with the authorities before you have any idea what you have been charged with can be dangerous. A day or two in a foreign slammer is no fun, but five years in a Third-World prison can spoil your whole trip.

If you hold an American Express card, the company can help locate an English-speaking lawyer. In the United States, the "Global Assist Hotline" can be reached at 1-800-544-AMEX. If overseas, call (202) 554-2639 (collect). This service can also be used to inform your family and employer of your situation.

In some foreign countries, even criminal cases can be resolved by "restitution." A reckless driving charge which results in somebody's cow being killed, for example, can sometimes be resolved by paying a fine and compensating the farmer for his loss. Such payment may greatly exceed the value of the cow, but time spent in a foreign hoosegow is irretrievably lost.

In any case, you should follow the consular officer's advice. He or she will try hard to get you out. If it appears you will be detained for some time, be aware that many foreign prison systems are "self-sustaining," that is, prisoners are expected to take care of themselves. If this is the case, have your family or company provide you with basic living necessities and barter goods for the period of your incarceration. Jail will still not be fun, but this will give you a better chance of living through it.

DRUGS

Every year thousands of Americans are arrested overseas for drug possession. Foreign laws with regard to even small quantities of drugs can be much more draconian than in the United States. It is a felony in some countries to have as much as one-tenth of a gram of cocaine or one marijuana cigarette. If you are apprehended and accused of drug use, the U.S. consular office can do very little for you except:

- visit you in jail after being notified of your arrest,
- give you a list of local attorneys,
- notify your family or friends and request money and other aid—but only with your authorization,
- intercede with local authorities to make sure your rights *under local law* are observed and that you are treated humanely, and
- protest mistreatment (e.g., torture) to the appropriate authorities.

The U.S. consular officer *cannot* demand your release or get you out of jail, represent you at trial or provide legal counsel, or pay legal fees or fines with U.S. government funds.

Drug offenses are regarded so seriously overseas that even basic constitutional protections we take for granted are simply not available. Penalties can include anything up to the death sentence in some countries, including Saudi Arabia, Malaysia, Singapore, Turkey, and Thailand. There is no such thing as recreational use of drugs overseas.

HIJACKING/HOSTAGE SITUATIONS

The U.S. State Department has issued the following advice concerning hijacking or hostage taking.

While every hostage situation is different and the chance of becoming a hostage is remote, some considerations are important. The U.S. government's policy not to negotiate with terrorists is firm—doing so only increases the risk of further hostage taking by terrorists. When Americans are abducted overseas, we [the U.S. government] look to the host government to exercise its responsibility under international law to protect all persons within its territories and to bring about the safe release of the hostages. We [the U.S. government] work closely with these governments from the outset of a hostage-taking incident to insure that our citizens and other innocent victims are released as quickly and safely as possible.

The most dangerous phases of most hijacking or hostage situations are the beginning and, if there is a rescue attempt, the end. At the outset the terrorists particularly are tense and high-strung and may behave irrationally. It is extremely important that you remain calm and alert and manage your own behavior.

- Avoid resistance and sudden or threatening movements. Do not struggle or try to escape unless you are *certain* of being successful.
- Make a concerted effort to relax. Breathe deeply and prepare yourself mentally, physically, and emotionally for the possibility of a long ordeal.
- Try to remain inconspicuous; avoid direct eye contact and the appearance of observing your captors' actions.
- Avoid alcoholic beverages. Consume little food and drink.
- Consciously put yourself in a mode of passive cooperation. Talk normally. Do not complain. Avoid belligerency, and comply with all orders and instructions.
- If questioned, keep your answers short. Don't volunteer information or make unnecessary overtures.
- Do not try to be a hero, endangering yourself and others.

- Maintain your sense of personal dignity, and gradually increase your requests for personal comforts. Make these requests in a reasonable, low-key manner.
- If you are engaged in a lengthier, drawn-out situation, try to establish a rapport with your captors, avoiding political discussions or other confrontational subjects.
- Establish a daily program of mental and physical activity. Don't be afraid to ask for anything you need or want—medicines, books, pencils, papers.
- Eat what they give you, even if it does not look or taste appetizing. A loss of appetite and weight is normal.
- Think positively; avoid a sense of despair. Rely on your inner resources. Remember that you are a valuable commodity to your captors. It is important to them to keep you alive and well.*

To these comforting words from the U.S. government might be added the following:

1. If traveling in areas where hostage taking is prevalent, you should not carry U.S. military identification unless it is absolutely necessary. Reservists, National Guard members, etc. should leave their military IDs at home unless the ID is required for the purposes of their trip.
   a. Stay fit. A daily regimen of exercise (even isometrics) will not only keep you prepared for sudden action should that become necessary but provides good mental discipline as well.
   b. If you are going to be traveling in areas where hostage taking is prevalent, leave instructions for your family and business as to how you would like them to react to a hostage situation. Sometimes, families and business acquaintances have done more harm than good in negotiating the release of hostages abroad.
   c. Request a copy of a Bible, Koran, or other scriptures. Often, hostage-taking situations involve religious fanati-

* *A Safe Trip Abroad*, United States Department of State, Bureau of Consular Affairs, Publication 9493.

cism. Not only will hostage takers often be more reluctant to injure individuals actively studying a religion, you might even learn something.

DUAL NATIONALS

American citizens who are dual nationals sometimes have a difficult time in troubled areas. A foreign country might claim you as a citizen if you were born there or your parents were or are citizens of that country, or if you are a naturalized U.S. citizen. If you are in any of the above categories, consult the embassy of the country you are planning to visit.

While recognizing the existence of dual nationality, the U.S. government does not encourage it because of the problems it may cause. Claims of other countries upon dual-national U.S. citizens often place them in situations where their obligations to one country conflict with U.S. law. Dual nationality may hamper efforts by the U.S. government to provide diplomatic and consular protection. When a U.S. citizen is in the other country of his or her dual nationality, that country has a predominant claim on that person.

If you have questions about dual nationality, contact the nearest foreign service post or the Office of Citizens Consular Services, Bureau of Consular Affairs, Room 4817, Department of State, Washington, DC 20520.

12

Business Hints

Foreign business travel differs from travel within the United States in a number of ways. Not only are there language problems to contend with, but foreign business conditions often present difficulties you do not encounter at home. The following suggestions will help to make the trip more pleasant and productive.

TELEPHONES

In most foreign countries, outbound telephone calls are significantly more expensive than equivalent inbound calls from the United States. Therefore, it is advisable for your office to call you rather than you calling them. This can be done either by setting up a schedule for phoning or by making a short call to your office to advise them of where you are and what your telephone number is. When they call you back and you conclude your conversation, have your office switch you to other calls in the United States if possible. There is often an outrageous charge for each separate call from a foreign country; you can save money by merely having your calls forwarded.

Foreign hotels also impose surcharges on outgoing long-distance calls. These charges, together with normal tolls, can easily total more than your entire hotel bill.

One way to avoid some of the fees is to use U.S.A. Direct. This is a special number accessible from many foreign countries which allows you to call a local number and be billed at lower rates. There are two types of countries in which U.S.A. Direct is available: Dial Access Countries, from which you can use the service from any telephone, and Designated Telephone Countries. In the latter nations, you must look for specially marked telephones in major airports, hotels, cruise ports, and telephone centers and on U.S. military bases and fleet centers. This is a service of AT&T; you can pay for the service with an AT&T card or you can reverse the charges by calling collect.

Both types of countries are listed in appendix 8. Further information about this service can also be found by calling 800-874-4000, Extension 359. When you are overseas, call collect (412) 553-7458.

COURTESY/CUSTOMS

Common courtesy is relatively universal, but many foreign countries have special cultural and religious taboos which should be conscientiously avoided when abroad. As previously noted, unless you are already intimately familiar with the local customs, you should make a special effort to learn appropriate etiquette in the country you are visiting. There are a number of good books dealing with this; among the best are *Do's and Taboos around the World* by Roger Axtell, and the InterAct series (see the Bibliography).

If you are still uncertain about appropriate behavior, observe your hosts carefully and emulate their example. A word of caution: some cultures assign different etiquette to men and women. At some Jewish functions, for example, male participants may be offered yarmulke to wear, while women will not.

RECEIPTS

Try to keep all of your receipts in an envelope. Many, of course, will be written in a foreign language with no indication of exchange rate and sometimes without other pertinent data such as date, identification of purchase, etc. Before putting foreign receipts in your envelope, make notes on them adding whatever important data are missing. This will save considerable frustration when you seek reimbursement for receipts written in Hungarian. Foreign taxi drivers don't always offer receipts, so have them write the necessary information on a blank piece of paper and initial it. It is also important to retain receipts from banks where you have exchanged money to insure that you are reimbursed at the appropriate exchange rate.

BUSINESS CARDS

Business cards are absolutely essential when conducting business overseas. In addition to the standard information on American business cards, it is the custom in some foreign countries to list honorifics. Lawyers, for example, are often addressed as "Dr." In some countries university degrees are also indicated. In Asia it is important to give an indication of your rank or position in your company. Include your entire business title, spelled out completely, and telephone and telex numbers.

If you plan to spend significant time in a particular country, it might be worthwhile to have business cards printed in the language of that country on one side and in English on the other. When presenting your card, give it to your foreign business contact with the foreign-language side up. In Asia and the Middle East this should be done with the *right* hand or, in Japan, for instance, with both hands.

The Western tradition of accepting a business card and immediately putting it in your pocket is considered very rude in most Asian countries. The proper approach is to look carefully at the card after accepting it, observe the title and organization, acknowledge with a nod that you have digested the information and, perhaps, make a relevant comment or ask a polite question. During a meeting, spread the cards in front of you in relation to where people are sitting.

It is a major faux pas to mix up your cards in different languages. For example, if you had business cards printed in both Korean and Japanese, be sure you do not offer a Korean business executive your Japanese calling card.

TELEX/FACSIMILE

Although fax machines are growing in popularity around the world, many countries still rely on telex. Fortunately, you don't need a telex machine these days to have a telex number. Often, a computer modem will do. Check with Western Union for details.

COMPUTERS

Use of laptop computers is extremely popular in the United States but less so abroad. There are a number of factors to consider when you travel with a computer overseas.

Electric current. Foreign current is often different from the 110-volt/60-cycle current in the United States, and the AC/DC transformer you use at home may not work overseas. Worse yet, using your regular transformer overseas may cause serious damage to your computer. You should either get a transformer which can accept various voltages (the most common is 220-volt/50-cycle) or buy a voltage converter for use overseas. [Note: this is not merely an adapter for foreign plugs but an actual voltage converter which will convert the foreign current into 110-volt/60-cycle.] These usually come equipped with conversion plugs for foreign electrical outlets. If your U.S. transformer has a 3-prong plug, be sure it fits in the converter before you leave. It may be necessary to buy a 2-prong adapter.

Using a voltage converter overseas can sometimes disrupt the current in the hotel. This particularly affects television reception. If this is a problem, many foreign hotels will have a shaver outlet in the bathroom that has 110 volts. Using this outlet to charge your laptop reduces electrical interference caused by the converter. The transformer itself should not cause electrical interference.

When traveling overseas, have the batteries in your laptop computer constantly topped off. Frequent power outages in some countries mean you should take advantage of electricity when you can. Be aware, however, that the most efficient way of charging batteries is to allow them to entirely deplete, then charge them fully. This contradiction can only be resolved on the scene. If blackouts are frequent, charge your computer whenever you can. If they are seldom, charge when you are reasonably sure you will have six or seven hours of power.

Modems. Many foreign countries have not yet adopted the kind of telephone plugs now standard in the U.S. Further, many foreign hotels "hard wire" telephones into the wall so you cannot merely plug your computer in to the telephone socket. Since using your modem then becomes a problem, it is a good idea to have an acoustic coupler. This can be purchased at most computer supply stores. Acoustic couplers are subject to interference so you should use the minimum baud rate. Foreign telephone mouthpieces are also not identical to American ones, so get a flexible coupler.

Many foreign telephone systems still use pulse dialing as opposed to the touch tone dialing used in the United States, but all major communications software has a pulse mode. Find out how to use it before you leave. When using pulse dialing, it is often advisable to insert a pause after each number dialed, as the antiquated phone systems in some countries have difficulty if the computer "speaks" too fast.

In some countries, transmission of encrypted messages is prohibited. Check on the existence of such regulations before using your modem. Some nations have U.S. export restrictions even covering laptop computers for your personal use. Check with the U.S. Department of Commerce Export Administration before you leave with regard to current restrictions.

You should note that downloading information onto your laptop computer from a foreign data base is sometimes difficult, particularly in developing countries, because of interference in phone lines. This can sometimes be corrected by lowering the baud transmission rate (if possible) or by disassembling the telephone and connecting it by direct coupling rather than using an acoustic coupler. If you are traveling to a Third-World country, learn how to do these tasks before you leave; computer technicians are sometimes scarce.

Printers. If you take your laptop computer with you, take along a portable printer and an extra ink cartridge. Although in the United States it is relatively easy to hook up your laptop to readily available printers, these devices are not ubiquitous overseas. Further, foreign printers are sometimes incompatible with the laptop you may have.

Having a computer with a printer is particularly useful in negotiations. Hard copies of contracts can be prepared and actually signed on the spot rather than sent afterward. But don't demand or even expect to get signatures this quickly; in many countries a slower negotiation process is a cultural imperative.

FOREIGN TOILETS

Americans traveling abroad are frequently put off by foreign toilets, even in highly industrialized countries. The smells, lack of cleanliness, and unfamiliar construction of many toilets are often very upsetting. Americans are further annoyed when they have to pay for the use of toilets which *are* decent.

Cultures differ in the value they place on many things, including the nature of their bathroom facilities. Americans and the Japanese are at one end of the spectrum, expecting a high degree of cleanliness, comfort, and odorlessness. Other cultures are less concerned about the conditions in which bodily needs are met, stressing more such things as the quality of the food and wine they consume or close human relationships in an extended family system.

Further, there are a number of American behaviors which many foreigners find just as unpleasant as Americans find foreign toilets: the American habit, for instance, of blowing one's nose into a handkerchief and then storing the handkerchief in a pocket or the practice of sitting in a tub of water saturated with the dirt one has just washed from one's body.

The point, of course, is that one deals with differences in bathroom facilities while abroad the same way one deals with other differences—by adapting to them and keeping one's complaint to oneself. Here are some of the best ways to adapt American fastidiousness to foreign realities.

1. Facilities are generally better where there is an attendant or where you otherwise have to pay or leave a tip. Look for these places and don't begrudge the payment.
2. Bring your own accessories (i.e., facial tissue, toilet paper, soap, washcloth) with you in a plastic bag in your briefcase.
3. Use the facilities before leaving your hotel, where they are

almost certain to be more acceptable to you than those you will encounter elsewhere.

Do not judge other cultures by the quality of their toilets. You will miss much if you do, and you are likely to project an image of an especially ugly American.

GIFTS

In most foreign countries gifts are not only appreciated but expected. These generally need not be elaborate, but they provide you with an opportunity to promote your firm. Gifts with your corporate logo (pens, lighters, money clips, paperweights, etc.) are often appropriate. Alternatively, gifts which represent your region of the country are appreciated (e.g., wild rice from Minnesota, peanuts from Virginia, maple syrup from Vermont, etc.). Do not give any gift which is easily accessible and implies that the recipient could not get it for herself or himself.

Customs concerning gift giving are important to understand. In some cultures, gifts are expected and failure to present them is considered an insult, while in others, offering a gift is considered offensive. Business executives also need to know when to present gifts (on the initial visit or afterward), where to present them (in public or private), what types are appropriate, what color they should be (or, more important, *not* be), how many to present, and to whom they should be presented.

If you are giving gifts to more than one person at the same time, it is particularly important to recognize the rank of the recipient, especially in East Asia. Giving the same gift to everyone you meet can be regarded as offensive, particularly if it is done in a public place. As previously noted, Axtell's *Do's and Taboos around the World* is helpful on this subject.

In certain countries, gifts of what Americans regard as mundane are particularly appreciated, such as coffee beans (but not canned coffee), cognac, bourbon, or whiskey—liquor is especially valued in Japan. Samples of company products are sometimes appropriate. In the case of industrial products, models of them will certainly be displayed in the recipient's office. Creativity in gift giving, when in good taste, is often helpful in distinguishing your company. One major American company has its sales representatives request two business cards from their foreign contacts. One is later laminated into a luggage tag with the American company's corporate logo on one side and the foreign contact's business card on the other. It makes a unique thank-you gift sent as a follow-up.

GUIDEBOOKS AND MAPS

Business travelers should not overlook tourist guidebooks for their countries of destination. These books not only contain information on tourist attractions but also useful information concerning language, culture, history, restaurants, and hotels. Some of the most popular guidebooks are country-specific editions by such publishers as Baedecker, Berlitz, Birnbaums, Blue Guide, Fielding, Fodor, Gault Millay, Insight, Lonely Planet, and Michelin.

In some countries, accurate maps are not readily available. You should secure maps of countries and cities you will be visiting before leaving the United States.

PHOTOGRAPHY

Photography is generally encouraged in most countries. However, as discussed in chapter 11 (page 73), many governments prohibit the photographing of military installations or locations having military significance, including airports, bridges, tunnels, port facilities, and public buildings. Information on restrictions can be obtained from local tourist offices or from the nearest U.S. embassy or consulate. Taking photographs of such subjects without prior permission can result in your arrest or the confiscation of your camera and/or film.

AIR EXPRESS

When traveling overseas, carry some preaddressed, prepaid air express plastic packets for mailing dictated messages, computer disks, notes, etc., back to the office. Although the concierge in most hotels will take care of dispatching Federal Express and DHL or UPS, it is sometimes better to do it yourself. DHL, UPS and Federal Express offices are usually listed in the local telephone book, or you can call any of the major services before you leave for the names and addresses of their foreign offices.

GATHERING INFORMATION

In addition to gathering specific information on markets and other business and economic data, make sure to familiarize yourself with general information on the political and economic conditions of the country concerned. This is not difficult; political, economic, and agricultural profiles are available from the U.S. State Department, the U.S. Commerce Department, and the U.S. Department of Agriculture.

The State Department publishes *Background Notes,* brief flyers describing most countries of the world. There are about 170 *Notes* containing the most current information on people, culture, geography, history, government, economy, and political conditions. *Background Notes* also include a reading list, travel notes, and maps. Single copies are available from the U.S. Government Printing Office by calling (202) 783-3238.

The U.S. and Foreign Commercial Service (FCS) maintains offices in sixty-eight American and 122 foreign cities and offers numerous publications. Contact your local district office for information on what is available. Lists of overseas U.S. and FCS offices are included in appendixes 1 and 2.

The U.S. Department of Commerce also publishes a biweekly magazine, *Business America* (listed in the Bibliography). This is a useful publication for catching up with the latest programs, including trade fairs and overseas business opportunities.

The Foreign Agricultural Service (FAS) publishes dozens of pamphlets, market profiles, and fact sheets on international trade in agricultural products. To obtain a list of its publications, contact the Information Division, Room 5920 South Building FAS, USDA, Washington, DC 20250-1000. Request the free pamphlet, *How to Get Information on U.S. Agricultural Trade.*

LAUNDRY

Business travelers should consider having their laundry done every day. Foreign holidays are sometimes unpredictable and delivery schedules erratic. As soon as you arrive in a foreign country, send out the clothes in which you arrived, and do so every day thereafter until two days before your next departure. It costs no more to use this service daily and can save considerable embarrassment.

WAKE-UP CALLS

Your business schedule should not be trusted to wake-up calls from hotel operators. Not only are there language difficulties, but the shift usually changes by the time you are scheduled to receive your call and messages have an eerie way of getting lost. Bring a travel alarm clock, and use the telephone wake-up call service only as a backup. If purchasing an alarm clock, buy one which indicates world time zones. It can be helpful in determining the timing of international calls.

VIDEOTAPES

If you take demonstration videotapes overseas, they must obviously be compatible with the system used by the country in which you are traveling. The three major systems are NTSC, PAL, and SECAM (the U.S. uses NTSC). Check before you leave with the embassy of the country you are visiting to see which system that country uses and have your demonstration tapes formatted to the appropriate system before you go.

ELECTRICAL ADAPTERS

Many hotels overseas will have a 110-220 outlet in the bathroom. As noted earlier in this chapter, these are usually marked for shavers, but they can be used for other purposes as well, such as recharging batteries and laptop computers. Do not, however, attempt to use hair dryers or similar appliances in these outlets. The shaver plug will generally accept American-style plugs, but be careful. On many newer American appliances, one of the prongs will be slightly wider than the other and will not fit in these shaver receptacles; bring your adapters with you.

ESSENTIAL CARDS

Experienced business travelers often carry a laminated card in their wallet with the following information: passport number, date, and place of issue; insurance policy number (and issuing company); and frequent flyer number(s). Keep a "one-time" card in your wallet with your airline ticket number (in case you have to replace lost tickets) and refund service number as well as the serial numbers of traveler's checks.

13

Traveling In-Country

Traveling within a foreign country involves different rules from those which apply at home and can often be frustrating. This chapter will consider some of the things you can do to make in-country trips more pleasant.

GETTING AROUND

Although it may appear unglamorous, getting around in many cities is much faster by public transit than by taxi. This is especially true in those cities which have subways. Subway systems are almost always well marked and easily understandable to foreigners, even if you don't speak the language, and they are often far superior both in speed and in price to taxi service. While buses can be somewhat more problematic, they are also a viable means of transportation. A local bus used with a well-written guidebook can be one of the biggest bargains around.

BY AIR

In many foreign countries, the local air carriers have a monopoly. The virtues of competition are never more apparent than in this situation; local airlines in such cases usually offer abominable service. If possible, book your internal travel plans before you leave the U.S. Local air carriers are much more accommodating to foreign travel agencies (and airlines) than they are to their own citizens.

If you are required to buy a ticket locally, check first with your hotel concierge to see if the hotel can arrange its purchase, then check with American Express or another local travel agent. If all else fails, you may be forced to go to the local airline office to buy your own, which can be very slow and inefficient. Sometimes an indication of your willingness to pay for your ticket in hard currency can put you at the front of the line; other times it will not. These airlines often write domestic tickets by hand, having diverted their computer resources to international travelers. Be persistent—and patient. You should also realize that a "confirmed" notation on your ticket does not mean confirmed in the Western sense. Some business travelers have been known to slip the booking agent a ten-dollar bill for a local confirmation to improve their chances of having the "OK" notice on their tickets really mean something. Be careful, though, where you try this trick; in some countries it sometimes works if you are firm and persistent; in others it is highly insulting.

BY TRAIN

In many foreign countries, including the developing countries, rail travel is far easier, cheaper, and faster than any other mode of transportation and is often superior to that found in the United States. Here are some tips that will help to make your trip easier.

Getting your ticket: Often, travel agents will not be able to get overseas train tickets for you. Even when you are in the country where you intend to travel by rail, travel agents sometimes defer to the railroad themselves. Generally, you will have to go to the train station to purchase your ticket.

Timetables: Before you leave for your trip, try to get train schedules. These are sometimes available commercially; the *Thomas Cook Continental Timetable* for European trains, for example, is available at many travel agencies. Timetables are also available at the train stations themselves, though they will not be in English in non-English speaking countries. Also, because of abbreviations, you may need some help in deciphering the hieroglyphics of foreign timetables. But once you understand the parlance, reading timetables is easy. Pay particular attention to public holidays. While trains may still run, service is usually curtailed and schedules are delayed.

Twenty-four-hour time: Most foreign train timetables are written on the basis of a twenty-four-hour clock (also known as military time) numbered consecutively from 0 to 24, starting at midnight. A train arriving at midnight is shown as "24.00." A train leaving at midnight is shown as "0.00." Arrivals and departures between midnight and 1:00 A.M. are indicated as "0.01" to "0.59." One of the most common causes of missed trains is misreading these times and arriving a day early or a day late.

Accommodations: Foreign train travel offers a bewildering number of options for accommodations. There are usually two or three classes of service, designated most commonly as *third class, second class,* and *first class.* This is called *base ticketing.*

Third class passengers usually ride in a compartment with four or five other people or all together on hard benches, often with goats and chickens too. First and second class passengers sometimes have additional options. Many overnight trains, for instance, offer a choice between couchettes and sleepers. Couchettes are simply mixed-sex sleeping compartments with berths (four in first class, six in second). Sheets, blankets, and pillows are sometimes provided; if not, you simply sleep on the wooden shelf. There are no private washing facilities, though some of the more luxurious sleeping cars may have washbasins with hot and cold water and air conditioning. With a first class ticket you may be offered the choice between a sleeper, a coach special (which is slightly smaller), or a large double with a king-sized bed. These options will be added to your ticket, or you may be given separate coupons for them.

Tickets: In many countries one train ticket is issued for a group of people traveling together. Reserved seats, couchettes, or sleepers are generally recorded on separate vouchers or coupons, which are stapled to the base ticket. Each ticket indicates the destination and includes the date and time of arrival (according to the twenty-four-hour clock); class; number of the coach on the train; number of the train; and number of the seat, berth, or compartment. It can be quite confusing, so learn how to read your ticket before you board the train. Some people spend half the journey walking up and down the aisle looking for their seat because they are unable to decipher the ticket. If your journey has several segments and you want a reserved seat, try to book it for the whole way.

Double booking: If you board the train and it appears your reservations have been double-booked, stand your ground; call an attendant, even if others are already in possession of the compartment. Sleeping-car attendants have been known to take bribes to get people on trains that are already full. If both you and the other party have what seem to be genuine tickets, the attendant will probably put one of you into a sleeper being held for someone further up the line in the hope that he or she does not turn up. Except in these circumstances, do not worry if the attendant disappears with your tickets—even overnight. This is a quite normal practice on long-distance trains, and by leaving your passports with the attendant, you may escape the discomfort of being awakened when the train crosses a frontier.

Date stamping. In some countries, such as France, you should date-stamp your ticket when leaving the station to board the train at the departure point. This is usually done by machine. If you fail to date-stamp it, the conductor could charge you a premium.

Excursions: Stay close to your compartment during your journey. Foreign trains are decoupled at odd hours, and you could find yourself heading on a separate route from the one you intended if you are in another car which is then attached to a different train. Train stops will usually be announced either over a loudspeaker or by a car attendant. Listen carefully to these announcements and know how to pronounce your destination in the local language so you won't miss your stop.

BY CAR

One of the best ways for a business traveler to get around in a foreign country is by car. Many U.S. rental companies have agencies overseas. If you are considering renting a car abroad, there are several things you need to know:

1. Classes and types of cars overseas differ from their U.S. counterparts. The cars themselves may also be unfamiliar, and rate schedules are almost certain to be different. The classification of car size and quality—compacts or luxury in the U.S.—are often stated in terms of alphabetical denominations abroad (A, B, C, etc.).

2. Foreign affiliates of U.S. rental companies sometimes do not honor U.S.-issued coupons or "specials" for lower rates; often, they are merely franchise operations.

3. Unlike renting a car in the U.S., it is a good idea to accept the insurance offered by the foreign rental company. A prudent business traveler should always take maximum liability coverage including a collision damage waiver when renting a car overseas. Some insurance policies offered by rental companies will not cover you if you leave the country in which you rented the car. If additional insurance is necessary, ask the rental company how to procure it.

4. Although a valid U.S. driver's license is generally sufficient to rent a car in most overseas rental locations, you should also get an International Driving Permit (IDP). It can save considerable embarrassment and delay if you are involved in an accident. You can purchase a permit (valid for one year) through the American Automobile Association.

5. Foreign rental cars will be accompanied by documentation (title, insurance documents, etc.). You will find these in the glove compartment of the car, or they may be given to you when you rent the car. You must have these documents with you at all times when driving the car, particularly when crossing international borders. Foreign police routinely spot-check drivers for them. When you park overnight, take them with you. Often, car thieves will look for appropriate documentation in the car before they figure it is worth stealing. Having

the documents with you is not an absolute deterrent to theft, but it will help the authorities to recover the car—and it helps to identify the car to the rental company.

6. Certain countries, such as Switzerland, require road permits in lieu of tolls for using their divided highways. Fines may be levied on drivers who have no permit. The embassies or consulates will know if the countries you plan to visit require permits. Car rental agencies should also be able to advise you whether road permits are necessary.

7. Random testing of motorists is widespread, and sometimes police will set up roadblocks to check every motorist for a variety of potential offenses. Always carry your passport, U.S. driver's license, IDP, car registration documents, and evidence of insurance. Anyone found without these may be immediately arrested; even motorists having only technical offenses, such as expired inspection stickers, have sometimes been forced to abandon their vehicles.

8. Foreign police often have sweeping powers to fine motorists on the spot. Even in those countries where local drivers are given tickets and are expected to pay fines at a later date, the police may levy "deposits" from visiting motorists to make certain they actually pay the fine before leaving the country. Carry sufficient local currency to pay such fines, or the car may be seized; traveler's checks and credit cards will not work.

Before you rip up any parking tickets you get, check the wheels. Many foreign countries have discovered the charm of the "Denver Boot"; vehicles are also frequently towed away.

In most countries, seat belts are compulsory, and many countries require safety devices such as warning triangles and first-aid kits. Ask your rental car agency about these requirements and check the trunk for the necessary equipment.

14

Visiting the Embassy

One of the first stops a business traveler should make when visiting a foreign country is the U.S. embassy. Most embassy personnel are delighted to see American business executives and can provide valuable insights into the local situation which can facilitate your trip in a variety of ways. The following suggestions will make your visit to the embassy more productive.

CALL IN ADVANCE

Embassy personnel have demanding schedules. A simple call or fax for an appointment is not only courteous but will make your visit much more worthwhile—and it will help you through security clearance. Sometimes appointments can be arranged before you leave home, but you should call to confirm them upon your arrival. A list of telephone numbers is included in appendix 3.

WHOM TO SEE

The first embassy official most business executives should contact is the U.S. and Foreign Commercial Service officer. U.S. and FCS officers are not employed by the Department of State (as are most other embassy officials) but by the U.S. Department of Commerce, and their function is to serve U.S. business interests abroad. U.S. and FCS officers are well positioned to advise business executives on local trading conditions and can provide a wealth of information concerning a country's financial position, business prospects, etc. The FCS officers can also help you arrange meetings with your local counterparts in both the government and private sectors. If you are considering hiring a local agent, discuss it with the FCS officer before you make the commitment. Although his or her opinions are not legally binding, FCS officers often have insights on the availability and competence of the local agents.

If you are dealing with agricultural exports or imports, see the representatives of the Foreign Agricultural Service. These are employees of the U.S. Department of Agriculture. In addition to being experts on local agricultural products and trade opportunities, they often have subspecialties in particular agricultural issues where their knowledge is very extensive and extremely valuable. They will be particularly anxious to encourage exports of U.S. agricultural products.

The economic counselor can provide general insights into economic conditions in the country. This is particularly useful in banking, insurance, and service industries. He or she can also help you deal with local financial institutions. Economic counselors are representatives of the Department of State and are generally Foreign Service Officers (FSOs). Their responsibilities are broader than either FAS or FCS officers, but they can provide a "big picture" analysis of the economy of an entire country.

The consular officer is a good person to know in any embassy even though these officers tend to come and go quite frequently. They can provide valuable in-country services and are the individuals you should contact in the event of an emergency. Having a friendly consular officer on your side is worthwhile if you anticipate trouble, or even if you don't.

ARRIVING AT THE EMBASSY

Because of terrorist attacks over the past ten years, the State Department has significantly beefed up security at most of its overseas posts. Outside the embassy you will generally be required to produce identification (typically a passport) and to identify the name of the officer(s) with whom you have an appointment. Most embassies have metal detectors; firearms are not allowed past this point.

The next stop will be a bullet-proof booth manned by an individual in the uniform of the United States Marine Corps. He will be firm but polite. He will also be armed. Listen carefully to what he says. He will confirm your appointment and ask for your passport. He will examine it and call the person with whom you wish to speak—and he will keep your passport. This is one circumstance in which you do not need to worry about being without your travel documents. Marines do not lose passports, nor is it likely that anyone would try to take one from them.

Someone will come to get you in the waiting room, where you will be given an identification pass to wear while in the embassy. Upon leaving, turn in your identification pass to the Marine guard, and he will give you back your passport.

If you have foreign business associates accompanying you to the embassy, make sure to introduce them to the Marine guard and to the person who comes to meet you. Often, foreigners are not permitted in restricted areas of American embassies, and it can save considerable embarrassment if the embassy is alerted to the impending arrival in advance.

MEETING EMBASSY OFFICIALS

Meetings with embassy officials should be kept as short as business meetings at home (half an hour is generally regarded as maximum). U.S. government officials stationed abroad—particularly FCS officers—will be delighted to accept promotional literature from visiting American business executives. Bring several copies of your materials. This literature is often displayed in the embassy library and can find its way to prospective business partners in a matter of weeks.

FOLLOW-UP

It is always advisable to write a thank-you letter to embassy officials whom you meet overseas. If you received extraordinary service, write to their superiors in Washington commending them. You may also wish to contact their superiors if you received truly discourteous service, but don't complain about nits. A complaint in an FAS, FSO, or FCS officer's file is poisonous and can wreck an entire career, so be judicious about going over the officer's head.

Stay in touch with people you met in the embassy via mail after you return. If you come out with a new product, inform them of it and put them on your regular mailing list. You would be amazed at how much these individuals appreciate recognition of their work and how much good they can do your company year round.

15

Traveling with Family

One of the rewards business executives may get for effective overseas travel is the clearance to bring their family along on the next trip. This is particularly true if you have been amassing frequent flyer points with the airlines. Bringing your family along on business trips should not be confused with a vacation, but it can make an extended trip overseas much more pleasant. There are a few things to consider when bringing your family on a business trip that are different from regular family vacations.

Frequent flyer clubs: Check your frequent flyer bonus status carefully. Rather than cashing in air miles for individual tickets, airlines often offer companion tickets at reduced prices. Frequent flyer clubs also have different schedules for the number of bonus miles it costs if one party purchases a full-fare ticket as opposed to two or more parties purchasing them.

Frequent flyer tickets sometimes have restrictions that full-fare tickets do not. Airlines allocate a number of seats on a particular aircraft which can be purchased with frequent flyer tickets, and blackout periods may apply. You may have to reschedule certain parts of your trip to take advantage of frequent flyer tickets because of the restrictions on your family's tickets.

Logistics: When you travel overseas with your family, follow the same rules as are outlined in prior chapters on traveling alone. Each person in your party should have a passport and appropriate visas.

Since there will probably be no one at home if you are traveling with your family, make appropriate arrangements with your office to pay your credit card and possibly other bills.

Protocol: In many countries, particularly Asia and parts of the Middle East, an invitation to dinner may not include the business executive's family. In fact, it is poor form to even suggest that they attend. If you make it known that your family is with you, an invitation may be volunteered, but it is rude to pressure your host.

Some business executives have business cards made for their children. These are merely calling cards with their address and telephone number. The children usually enjoy passing them out, and foreign adults, even though surprised, will tend to remember your children's names, and no local customs are likely to be violated. Be sure your spouse has both a card for himself or herself and carries your card as well. These come in handy at cocktail parties and other social gatherings.

Visiting the embassy: On at least one trip to the U.S. embassy, take your family with you. Often U.S. legations abroad don't see many families (particularly in Third-World countries) and are delighted to have Americans to talk to. This is especially true if you have children with you. There may even be some embassy children there. Particularly at small posts, children of embassy personnel often spend a lot of time at the embassy and will enjoy playing with your children.

Going to school: Even if you are going to be overseas for a short time, if you have foreign friends with school-age children, you may be able to arrange to have your children attend school for a day or two. Usually they are the object of some curiosity and will enjoy the experience. You might tell your children to bring some postcards from your home city or some other easy-to-carry American artifacts to show to the school that they may be visiting.

Identification: Although your spouse and older children should keep their passports with them at all times, it is normally better if you are responsible for the passports of very young children. The children should, however, have some form of identification on them at all times, including the name, address, and telephone number of your hotel. Write this information on a card together with the child's name, passport number, home address, and *your* name. Then pin the card on him or her or put it inside a buttoned or zippered pocket.

Children's purses or backpacks can be misplaced with a high degree of frequency, so be sure it is actually *on their person.*

Perspective: One of the major advantages of taking children overseas is to give them an opportunity to appreciate both their American lifestyle and those of other cultures, but prepare them before you arrive. Young children (under the age of twelve) are very perceptive, but they do not always have the ability to put their experiences into context. If you are traveling to a Third-World country, prepare all the children before you go for the poverty and disease they will probably observe, which may be shocking, especially to small children. They should also be told before they arrive in some countries about the increased presence of police and in some cases of soldiers with machine guns; the sight of heavily armed soldiers can be terrifying.

Restrictions on women and children: In some countries (especially those in Africa and the Middle East), either by law or by custom, a woman and her children need the husband's permission to leave the country. Find out about the laws and customs regarding women of the country you intend to visit and do not take your family unless you are certain they will be permitted to leave unhindered. Once overseas, you are subject to the laws of the country you are in; U.S. laws cannot protect you.

16 〜

Returning Home

Coming home is often the best part of an overseas business trip. But it can be more complicated than getting on an airplane bound for the United States. Here is some information, along with a few suggestions, that will make your homecoming easier and more enjoyable.

AT THE FOREIGN AIRPORT

At many foreign airports the local (or national) airline will be in charge of all luggage check-in. That is, rather than checking your bags with the airline desk as you would at a U.S. airport, you may be required to go to the local airline to check in on an American air carrier. Usually, there are signs to advise you of this. Allow yourself at least an hour and a half before flight time for checking in at foreign airports. They are often more crowded—and less efficient—than American international airports.

When checking in for your seat assignment and boarding pass—which will be at the airline you are actually flying on—inquire about departure taxes. Depending upon the country, you may be able to pay the departure taxes (sometimes called airport taxes) in local currency, or you may find that hard currency is required. Sometimes the tax can be paid at the check-in desk; other times you have to walk to a special kiosk where you must purchase a tax ticket or have your boarding pass stamped.

After you have checked your bags and paid your departure tax, exchange the rest of your local currency back into dollars at one of the airport banks or money exchanges (in many countries this is required). Have your original receipts handy to show to the exchange authorities. If you have excess local currency and no receipts to back it up, many countries will confiscate the balance of your local currency.

Unlike American airports, many foreign airports require you to pass through both customs and immigration upon departure. Fill out a departure form. Often, this will be the same form as your entry form, and it should have been put in your passport. If you have lost it, you will have to fill out another one.

The immigration/customs officers will ask to see your passport, visa, and boarding pass. Once you clear immigration formalities, you will be in the international departure area and may not return to the main terminal. At this point, your bags (depending upon the airport) may be examined numerous times. In some foreign airports, even after they have been examined, they will be placed on the tarmac by the steps to the plane and you must identify them again before you will be permitted to board the aircraft. Do not fail to do so. Unidentified bags are simply not put on the aircraft (or, alternatively, the plane will be delayed until they are identified). This is a protection against bombs, so be patient.

U.S. IMMIGRATION AND CUSTOMS

During your flight home, the flight attendants will give you a customs declaration form. Fill this out while you are still on the aircraft. When you go through immigration and customs at the U.S. port of entry, have your passport ready and your receipts of purchase handy in case you need to support your customs declaration. If you have packed the articles you acquired abroad separately, customs inspection will be easier. If you are returning to the U.S. by car from either Mexico or Canada, you should also have a Certificate of Vehicle Registration.

Articles acquired abroad are subject to duty *and* internal revenue tax. As a returning U.S. resident, you are allowed to bring back $400 worth of merchandise duty-free. However, you must have been outside the United States for at least forty-eight hours, and you must not have used this exemption within the preceding thirty-day period. The next $1,000 worth of items you bring back for personal use or gifts is subject to duty at a flat 10 percent rate.

RESTRICTIONS ON PRODUCTS
ENTERING THE U.S.

Before you depart for home, familiarize yourself with customs regulations and take note of prohibited categories. Many of these restrictions also apply to mailed products.

Products you will be prohibited from bringing into the United States include but are not limited to the following categories:

1. Pirated (unlawfully made) copies of copyrighted articles— books, records, computer programs, and cassettes. Pirated copies may be seized and either destroyed or returned to the country of export.

2. Cultural property, such as pre-Colombian monumental and architectural sculpture and murals (whether shipped directly or indirectly to the United States) may require an Export Certificate. Customs also enforces the Convention on Cultural Property Implementation Act, which prohibits illicit traffic in cultural property but does allow the exchange of national treasures for legitimate scientific, educational, and cultural purposes.

3. Narcotics, dangerous drugs (including anabolic steroids), and drug paraphernalia may be seized and the bearer subjected to criminal penalties.

4. Firearms and ammunition are subject to restrictions of the ATF. Applications to import may be made only by or through a licensed importer, dealer, or manufacturer. Weapons, ammunition, or devices prohibited by the National Firearms Act will not be admitted into the United States unless authorized by ATF. No import permit is required if you can show that you took the firearms or ammunition out of the United States with you (*see chapter 1* regarding licensing and registration of firearms).

5. Gold coins, metals, and bullion may be brought into the U.S., but *copies* of gold coins are prohibited if not properly marked.

6. The importation of merchandise or goods that contain components from the following countries are generally prohibited under regulations administered by the Office of Foreign Assets Control, U.S. Department of the Treasury: Cambodia,

Cuba, Iran, Libya, North Korea, Iraq, and Vietnam. There are no prohibitions on the import of communication materials such as pamphlets, books, tapes, films, or recordings. Specific licenses are required to bring prohibited merchandise into the United States, and they are rarely granted.

FOOD

Bringing fresh fruit, vegetables, plants (in soil), and many other agricultural products into the United States is prohibited because they may carry foreign insects and diseases that could damage U.S. crops, forests, gardens, and livestock.

Regulations additionally prohibit the importation of fresh, dried, and canned meat and meat products from most foreign countries. If any meat is used in preparing a product, it is prohibited. Commercially canned meat is allowed if the inspector can determine that the meat was cooked in the can after it was sealed to make it shelf-stable without refrigeration.

You will be required to declare any agricultural products when you enter the country, orally or in writing. Officers of USDA's Animal and Plant Health Inspection Service (APHIS) examine passenger baggage for undeclared agricultural products. At some ports they use beagles to sniff them out, while others use low-energy X ray machines adapted to reveal fruits and meats. These are quite effective; prohibited agricultural products confiscated have doubled in recent years, and an average of 1,250 violations are uncovered each month. The traveler who fails to declare a prohibited item is fined on the spot up to fifty dollars (or more), and the item is confiscated.

Although some agricultural products are admissible without advance permission (provided they are declared, inspected, and found free of pests), others require that you obtain a permit in advance. For more information, request the pamphlet, "Trip Tips on Bringing Food, Plant and Animal Products into the United States," available from the Agricultural Affairs Office of U.S. embassies abroad, or write to the Animal and Plant Health Inspection Service, U.S. Department of Agriculture, 732 Federal Building, 6505 Belcrest Road, Hyattsville, MD 20782.

ENDANGERED SPECIES

U.S. laws and international treaties make it a crime to bring back many endangered plants and animals into the United States, as well as articles made from these species. Some prohibited items include articles made from sea turtle shells, reptile skins, ivory, certain cat species, marine mammals, and coral reefs. Do not buy any kind of wildlife souvenirs if you are unsure of being able to bring them legally into the United States. The penalties are severe and your purchases will probably be confiscated.

To learn more about endangered wildlife and guidelines governing restrictions on imports, obtain the pamphlet, *Buyer Beware*, available free from the Publications Unit, U.S. Fish and Wildlife Service, Department of the Interior, Washington, DC 20240. Additional information on the importing of wildlife and wildlife products can be obtained through TRAFFIC (U.S.A.), World Wildlife Fund-U.S., 1250 24th Street, NW, Washington, DC 20037.

GLAZED CERAMICS

Although foreign glazed ceramics are not prohibited from entry into the United States, consider carefully the purchase of ceramic tableware and clay pottery overseas. The U.S. Food and Drug Administration has determined that there are dangerous levels of lead found in the glazes of some ceramic dinnerware and pottery sold abroad. Because there is no way of knowing whether a particular item is safe, the Food and Drug Administration recommends that you use such wares for decorative purposes only.

AUTOMOBILES

If you plan on purchasing an automobile overseas to bring back to the United States, there are a number of precautions to take. The Environmental Protection Agency (EPA) has established new rules effective for all vehicles imported after June 30, 1988, covering the importation of "nonconforming vehicles," which is any motor vehicle not manufactured to meet U.S. emissions standards. If a nonconforming vehicle is allowed entry into the United States, it must be modified within 120 days to meet the same EPA emissions standards that apply to vehicles built in the United States.

Only parties holding a valid Certificate of Conformity issued by the EPA are permitted to import nonconforming vehicles. The recipient of the certificate is authorized to import vehicles and modify them so they are within U.S. regulations. If you are considering importing a car, arrange to do so through a certificate holder. Not all vehicles are eligible for modification. Requirements vary with a vehicle's age and the qualifications of the certificate holder, so determine whether your car is eligible before you buy.

For information on vehicle importation requirements, see Other Resources.

Conclusion

All right. You have packed your bags, double-checked your travel documents, carefully observed security precautions, and confirmed all your bookings. You have also read this book cover to cover. Can anything go wrong? As they say in Minneapolis, "You bet."

You can vastly improve your odds by taking one additional precaution. Learn as much as possible about the history, culture, traditions, and politics of the countries you are visiting. Not only will this information improve the chances that your trip will be "glitchless," but it will enhance the probability that your business venture will be successful as well.

The Bibliography is a good place to start, but only a beginning. Talk to friends and colleagues who have been to the country. Meet with officials at the consulate closest to you. Bone up on at least a few phrases in the local language.

Most of all, check your own attitude. Foreign business travel need not be an unrelenting nightmare. It can be challenging, educational, and—I hope my boss doesn't read this—FUN!

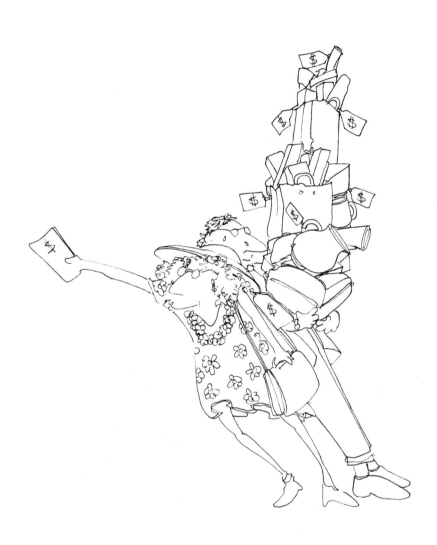

APPENDIX 1

U.S. and
Foreign Commercial Service
U.S. Offices

Birmingham
North Berry Building
2015 2nd Avenue North, Room 302
35203
(205) 731-1331

Anchorage
222 West 7th Avenue
PO Box 32
99513
(907) 271-5041

Phoenix
Federal Building & U.S. Courthouse
230 North 1st Avenue, Room 3412
85025
(602) 379-3285

ARKANSAS
Little Rock
Savers Federal Building
320 West Capitol Avenue, Suite 811
72201
(501) 378-5794

CALIFORNIA
Los Angeles
11000 Wilshire Boulevard, Room 9200
90024
(213) 575-7104

Santa Ana
116-A West 4th Street, Suite 1
92701
(714) 836-2461

San Diego
6363 Greenwich Drive, Suite 145
92122
(619) 557-5395

San Francisco
Federal Building
450 Golden Gate Avenue
PO Box 36013
94102
(415) 556-5860

COLORADO
Denver
680 World Trade Center
1625 Broadway
80202
(303) 844-3256

CONNECTICUT
Hartford
Federal Office Building
450 Main Street, Room 610-B
06103
(203) 240-3530

DELAWARE
Serviced by Philadelphia District Office

DISTRICT OF COLUMBIA
Washington, DC
(Baltimore, MD District)
Department of Commerce
14th Street & Constitution Avenue,
NW, Room 1066 HCHB
20230
(202) 377-3181

FLORIDA
Miami
Federal Building
51 SW First Avenue, Suite 224
33130
(305) 536-5267

Clearwater
128 North Osceola Avenue
34615
(813) 461-0011

Orlando
University of Central Florida
College of Business Administration
CEBA II, Room 346
32802
(407) 648-1608

Tallahassee
Collins Building
107 West Gaines Street, Room 401
32304
(904) 488-6469

GEORGIA
Atlanta
4360 Chamblee-Dunwoody Road
Suite 310
30341
(404) 452-9101

Savannah
120 Barnard Street, A-107
31401

HAWAII
Honolulu
4106 Federal Building
300 Ala Moana Boulevard
PO Box 50026
96850
(808) 541-1782

IDAHO
Boise
(Portland, OR District)
Hall of Mirrors Building
700 West State Street
83720
(208) 334-3857

ILLINOIS
Chicago
Mid-Continental Plaza Building
55 East Monroe Street, Room 1406
60603
(312) 353-4450

Palatine
W. R. Harper College
Algonquin & Roselle Roads
60067
(312) 397-3000, x2532

Rockford
> 515 North Court Street
> PO Box 1747
> 61110-0247
> (815) 987-8123

INDIANA
Indianapolis
> One North Capitol Avenue, Suite 520
> 46204
> (317) 226-6214

IOWA
Des Moines
> 817 Federal Building
> 210 Walnut Street
> 50309
> (515) 284-4222

Cedar Rapids
> 424 1st Avenue, NE
> 52401
> (319) 362-8418

KANSAS
Wichita
(Kansas City, MO District)
> River Park Place, Suite 580
> 727 North Waco
> 67203
> (316) 269-6160

KENTUCKY
Louisville
> Gene Snyder Courthouse and
> Customhouse Building
> 601 West Broadway, Room 636B
> 40202
> (502) 582-5066

LOUISIANA
New Orleans
432 World Trade Center
2 Canal Street
70130
(504) 589-6546

MAINE
Augusta
(Boston, MA District)
77 Sewall Street
04330
(207) 622-8249

MARYLAND
Baltimore
413 U.S. Customhouse
40 South Gay Street
21202
(301) 962-3560

MASSACHUSETTS
Boston
World Trade Center, Suite 307
Commonwealth Pier Area
02210
(617) 565-8563

MICHIGAN
Detroit
1140 McNamara Building
477 Michigan Avenue
48226
(313) 226-3650

Grand Rapids
300 Monroe NW, Room 406A
49503
(616) 456-2411

MINNESOTA
Minneapolis
108 Federal Building
110 South 4th Street
55401
(612) 348-1638

MISSISSIPPI
Jackson
328 Jackson Mall Office Center
300 Woodrow Wilson Boulevard
39213
(601) 965-4388

MISSOURI
Saint Louis
7911 Forsyth Boulevard, Suite 610
63105
(314) 425-3302

MONTANA
Serviced by Portland, OR District Office

NEBRASKA
Omaha
1133 "O" Street
68137
(402) 221-3664

NEVADA
Reno
1755 East Plumb Lane, #152
89502
(702) 784-5203

NEW HAMPSHIRE
Serviced by Boston District Office

NEW JERSEY
Trenton
3131 Princeton Pike Building, #6,
Suite 100
08648
(609) 989-2100

NEW MEXICO
Albuquerque
625 Silver, SW, Third Floor
87102
(505) 766-2070

Santa Fe
(Dallas, TX District)
c/o Economic Development
and Tourism Department
1100 Saint Francis Drive
87503
(505) 988-6261

NEW YORK
Buffalo
1312 Federal Building
111 West Huron Street
14202
(716) 846-4191

Rochester
111 East Avenue
Suite 220
14604
(716) 263-6480

New York
Federal Office Building
Foley Square
26 Federal Plaza, Room 3718
10278
(212) 264-0634

NORTH CAROLINA
Greensboro
324 West Market Street
PO Box 1950
27402
(919) 333-5345

NORTH DAKOTA
Serviced by Omaha District Office

OHIO
Cincinnati
9504 Federal Office Building
550 Main Street
45202

Cleveland
668 Euclid Avenue, Room 600
44114
(216) 522-4750

OKLAHOMA
Oklahoma City
6601 Broadway Extension
73116
(405) 231-5302

Tulsa
440 South Houston Street
74127
(918) 581-7650

OREGON
Portland
One World Trade Center
121 SW Salmon Street, Suite 242
97204
(503) 326-3001

PENNSYLVANIA
Philadelphia
475 Allendale Road, Suite 202
19406
(215) 962-4980

Pittsburgh
2002 Federal Building
1000 Liberty Avenue
15222
(412) 644-2850

PUERTO RICO
San Juan
Room G-55 Federal Building
00918
(809) 766-5555

RHODE ISLAND
Providence
(Boston, MA District)
7 Jackson Walkway
02903
(401) 528-5104

SOUTH CAROLINA
Columbia
Strom Thurmond Federal Building
1835 Assembly Street, Suite 172
29201
(803) 765-5345

Charleston
J. C. Long Building
9 Liberty Street, Room 128
29424
(803) 724-4361

SOUTH DAKOTA
Serviced by Omaha District Office

TENNESSEE
Nashville
Parkway Towers, Suite 1114
404 James Robertson Parkway
37219-1505
(615) 736-5151

Memphis
The Falls Building
22 North Front Street, Suite 200
38103
(901) 544-4137

TEXAS
Dallas
1100 Commerce Street, Room 7A5
75242
(214) 767-0542

Austin
816 Congress Avenue, Suite 1200
PO Box 12728
78711
(512) 482-5939

Houston
515 Rusk Street, Room 2625
77002
(713) 229-2578

UTAH
Salt Lake City
324 South State Street, Suite 105
84111
(801) 524-5116

VERMONT
Serviced by Boston District Office

VIRGINIA
Richmond
8010 Federal Building
400 North 8th Street
23240
(804) 771-2246

WASHINGTON
Seattle
3131 Elliott Avenue, Suite 290
98121
(206) 442-5616

Spokane
West 808 Spokane Falls Boulevard
Suite 650
99201
(509) 456-4557

WEST VIRGINIA
Charleston
3402 Federal Building
500 Quarrier Street
25301
(304) 347-5123

WISCONSIN
Milwaukee
Federal Building
U.S. Courthouse
517 East Wisconsin Avenue, Room 606
53202
(414) 297-3473

WYOMING
Serviced by Denver District Office

APPENDIX 2

Mailing Addresses of U.S. and Foreign Commercial Service Principal Overseas Posts

ALGERIA
American Embassy, SCO*
Algiers
U.S. Department of Commerce
Washington, DC 20230

ARGENTINA
American Embassy, SCO
Buenos Aires
APO Miami, FL 34034

AUSTRALIA
American Consulate General
Sydney
APO San Francisco, CA 96209

AUSTRIA
American Embassy, SCO
Vienna
APO New York, NY 09108

BARBADOS
American Embassy, SCO
Bridgetown
Box B
FPO Miami, FL 34054

BELGIUM
American Embassy, SCO
Brussels
APO New York, NY 09667

BRAZIL
American Embassy, SCO
Brasilia
APO Miami, FL 34030

CAMEROON
American Embassy, SCO
Yaounde
U.S. Department of Commerce
Washington, DC 20230

---

* For a list of current Senior Commercial Offices (SCOs), write to U.S. and Foreign Commercial Service, Department of Commerce, Washington, DC 20230.

131

CANADA
American Embassy, SCO
Ottawa
PO Box 5000
Ogdensburg, NY 13669

CHILE
American Embassy, SCO
Santiago
APO Miami, FL 34033

CHINA
American Embassy, SCO
Beijing
FPO San Francisco, CA 96655

COLOMBIA
American Embassy, SCO
Bogota
APO Miami, FL 34038

COSTA RICA
American Embassy, SCO
San Jose
APO Miami, FL 34020

CÔTE D'IVOIRE
American Embassy, SCO
Abidjan
U.S. Department of Commerce
Washington, DC 20230

DENMARK
American Embassy, SCO
Copenhagen
APO New York, NY 09170

DOMINICAN REPUBLIC
American Embassy, SCO
Santo Domingo
APO Miami, FL 34010

ECUADOR
American Embassy, SCO
Quito
APO Miami, FL 34039

EGYPT
American Embassy, SCO
Cairo
Box 11
FPO New York, NY 09527

FINLAND
American Embassy, SCO
Helsinki
APO New York, NY 09664

FRANCE
American Embassy, SCO
Paris
APO New York, NY 09777

U.S. Mission to the OECD
Paris SCO
APO New York, NY 09777

GERMANY
American Embassy, SCO
Bonn
Box 370
APO New York, NY 09080

GREECE
American Embassy, SCO
Athens
APO New York, NY 09255

GUATEMALA
American Embassy, SCO
Guatemala City
APO Miami, FL 34024

HONDURAS
American Embassy, SCO
Tegucigalpa
APO Miami, FL 34022

HONG KONG
American Consulate General
Hong Kong
Box 30
FPO San Francisco, CA 96659

HUNGARY
American Embassy, SCO
Budapest
APO New York, NY 09213

INDIA
American Embassy, SCO
New Delhi
U.S. Department of Commerce
Washington, DC 20230

INDONESIA
American Embassy, SCO
Jakarta
APO San Francisco, CA 96356

IRAQ
American Embassy, SCO
Baghdad
U.S. Department of Commerce
Washington, DC 20230

IRELAND
American Embassy, SCO
Dublin
U.S. Department of Commerce
Washington, DC 20230

ISRAEL
American Embassy, SCO
Tel Aviv
New York, NY 09672

ITALY
American Embassy, SCO
Rome
APO New York, NY 09794

JAMAICA
American Embassy, SCO
Kingston
U.S. Department of Commerce
Washington, DC 20230

JAPAN
American Embassy, SCO
Tokyo
APO San Francisco, CA 96503

KENYA
American Embassy, SCO
Nairobi
APO New York, NY 09675

KOREA
American Embassy, SCO
Seoul
APO San Francisco, CA 96301

KUWAIT
American Embassy, SCO
Kuwait City
U.S. Department of Commerce
Washington, DC 20230

MALAYSIA
American Embassy, SCO
Kuala Lumpur
U.S. Department of Commerce
Washington, DC 20230

MEXICO
American Embassy, SCO
Mexico City
PO Box 3087
Laredo, TX 78044

MOROCCO
American Consulate General
Casablanca
APO New York, NY 09284

NETHERLANDS
American Embassy, SCO
The Hague
APO New York, NY 09159

NEW ZEALAND
American Consulate General
Auckland
FPO San Francisco, CA 96690

NIGERIA
American Embassy, SCO
Lagos
U.S. Department of Commerce
Washington, DC 20230

NORWAY
American Embassy, SCO
Oslo
APO New York, NY 09085

PAKISTAN
American Consulate General
Karachi
APO New York, NY 09148

PANAMA
American Embassy, SCO
Panama
Box E
APO Miami, FL 34002

PERU
American Embassy, SCO
Lima
APO Miami, FL 34031

PHILIPPINES
American Embassy, SCO
Manila
APO San Francisco, CA 96528

POLAND
American Embassy, SCO
Warsaw
APO New York, NY 09213

PORTUGAL
American Embassy, SCO
Lisbon
APO New York, NY 09678

ROMANIA
American Embassy, SCO
Bucharest
APO New York, NY 09213

SAUDI ARABIA
American Embassy, SCO
Riyadh
APO New York, NY 09038

SINGAPORE
American Embassy, SCO
Singapore
APO San Francisco, CA 96699

SOUTH AFRICA
American Consulate General
Johannesburg
U.S. Department of Commerce
Washington, DC 20239

SPAIN
American Embassy, SCO
Madrid
APO New York, NY 09285

SWEDEN
American Embassy, SCO
Stockholm
U.S. Department of Commerce
Washington, DC 20230

SWITZERLAND
American Embassy, SCO
Bern
U.S. Department of Commerce
Washington, DC 20230

U.S. Mission to GATT
Geneva
U.S. Department of Commerce
Washington, DC 20230

TAIWAN
(An important non-US & FCS
commercial office)
American Institute in Taiwan
Taipei
Commercial Unit
PO Box 1612
Washington, DC 20013

THAILAND
American Embassy, SCO
Bangkok
APO San Francisco, CA 96346

TRINIDAD & TOBAGO
American Embassy, SCO
Port of Spain
U.S. Department of Commerce
Washington, DC 20230

TURKEY
American Embassy, SCO
Ankara
APO New York, NY 09257

UNITED ARAB EMIRATES
American Embassy, SCO
Abu Dhabi
U.S. Department of Commerce
Washington, DC 20230

UNITED KINGDOM
American Embassy, SCO
London
Box 40
FPO New York, NY 09509

URUGUAY
American Embassy
Montevideo (E)
Aluro Muller 1776
APO Miami, FL 34035

RUSSIAN FEDERATION
American Embassy, SCO
Moscow
APO New York, NY 09862

VENEZUELA
American Embassy, SCO
Caracas
APO Miami, FL 34037

YUGOSLAVIA
American Embassy, SCO
Belgrade
APO New York, NY 09213

APPENDIX 3 🙵

Street Addresses and Phone Numbers of U. S. Embassies Overseas

ALGERIA
Algiers
4 Chemin Cheikh Bachir Brahimi
Tel. (2) 601-425

ARGENTINA
Buenos Aires
4300 Columbia
Tel. (1) 774-7611

ARMENIA
Yerevan
Hotel Hrazdan
Tel. (7) (885) 2125-1144

AUSTRALIA
Canberra
Moonah Place
Tel. (62) 705000

AZERBAIJAN
Baku
Hotel Intourist
Tel. (7) (8922) 91-79-56

AUSTRIA
Vienna
Blotzmanngasse 16
Tel. (222) 31-55-11

BAHAMAS
Nassau
Mosmar Building
Queen Street
Tel. (809) 322-1181

BAHRAIN
Manama
Sheikh Isa Road
Tel. 714151

BELGIUM
Brussels
27 Boulevard du Régent
Tel. (2) 513-3830

BOLIVIA
La Paz
Calles Mercado y Colon
Tel. (2) 35-02-51

BRAZIL
Brasilia
Avenida das Naç es
Tel. (61) 321-7272

BULGARIA
Sofia
Boulevard Stamboliiski 1A
Tel. (2) 884-801

CANADA
Ottawa
100 Wellington Street
Tel. (613) 238-5335

CHILE
Santiago
Augustinas 1343
Tel. (2) 71-01-33

CHINA
Beijing
Xiu Shui Bei Jie #3
Tel. (1) 532-3831

COLOMBIA
Bogota
Calle 38, Número 8-61
Tel. (1) 285-1300

COSTA RICA
Pavas, San Jose
Tel. 20-39-39

CZECHOSLOVAKIA
Prague
Triziste 15-12548 Praha
Tel. (2) 53-6641

DENMARK
Copenhagen
Dag Hammarskjolds
Alle 24
Tel. (31) 42-31-44

ECUADOR
Quito
Avenida de la Patria, 12
Tel. (2) 562-890

EGYPT
Cairo
Lazouqi St
Garden City
Cairo
Tel. (2) 355-7371

FINLAND
Helsinki
Itainen Puistotie 14A
Tel. (0) 171-931

FRANCE
Paris
2 Avenue Gabriel
Tel. (1) 42-96-12-02

GEORGIA
Tbilisi
#25 Antonelli
Tel. (7) (883) 74-46-23

GERMANY
Bonn
Deichmanns Avenue 5300
Tel. (228) 3391

GREECE
Athens
91 Vassilissis Sophias Boulevard
Tel. (1) 721-2951

HONG KONG
Hong Kong
26 Garden Road
Tel. (5) 239011

HUNGARY
Budapest
V. Szabadsag Ter 12
Tel. (1) 112-6450

ICELAND
Reykjavik
Laufasvegur 21
Tel. (1) 29100

INDIA
New Delhi
Shanti Path
Chanakyapuri 110021
Tel. (11) 600651

INDONESIA
Jakarta
5 Merdeka Selatan
Tel. (21) 360360

IRELAND
Dublin
42 Elgin Road
Ballsbridge
Tel. (1) 687122

ISRAEL
Tel Aviv
71 Hayarkon Street
Tel. (3) 654338

ITALY
Rome
Via Veneto 119/A
Tel. (6) 46741

JAPAN
Tokyo
10-1 Akasaka,
Minato-Ku
Tel. (33) 224-5000

JORDAN
Amman
Jebel Amman
Tel. (6) 644371

KAZAKHSTAN
Alma-Ata
Seyfullina Building
Tel. (7) (3272) 62-13-75

KENYA
Nairobi
Haile Selassie Avenue
Tel. (2) 334141

KOREA
Seoul
82 Sejonj-Ro
Tel. (2) 732-2601

KUWAIT
Kuwait City
13001 Safat
Tel. 242-41-51

KYRGYZSTAN
Bishkek
#66 Erkindic
Tel. (7) (3312) 22-22-70

LEBANON
Beirut
Antelias
Tel. 417774

LUXEMBOURG
Luxembourg
22 Boulevard Emmanuel-Servais
Tel. 460123

MALAYSIA
Kuala Lumpur
376 Jalan Tun Razak
Tel. (03) 248-9011

MEXICO
Mexico City
Paseo de la Reforma
Tel. (5) 211-0042

MINSK
Byelarus
#46 Starovilenskaya
Tel. (7) (0172) 69-08-02

MOLDOVA
Chisinau
103 Strada Alexei Mateevich
Tel. (7) (0442) 23-28-94

MOROCCO
Rabat
2 Avenue de Marrakech
Tel. (7) 622-65

NETHERLANDS
The Hague
Lange Voorhout 102
Tel. (70) 62-49-11

NEW ZEALAND
Wellington
29 Fitzherbert Ter.
Tel. (4) 722-068

NIGERIA
Lagos
2 Eleke Crescent
Tel. (1) 610097

NORWAY
Oslo
Drammensveien 18
Tel. (2) 44-85-50

PAKISTAN
Islamabad
Diplomatic Enclave
Tel. (51) 8261-61

PANAMA
Panama City
Avenida Balboa,
entre Calles 37 y 38
Tel. 27-1777

PARAGUAY
Asuncion
1776 Mariscal
Lopez Avenida
Tel. (21) 201-041

PERU
Lima
Avenidas I. G. de la Vega y
    Espana
Tel. (14) 338-000

PHILIPPINES
Manila
1201 Roxas Boulevard
Tel. (2) 521-71-16

POLAND
Warsaw
Aleje Ujazdowskie 29/31
Tel. (22) 283041

PORTUGAL
Lisbon
Avenue das F. Armadas
Tel. (1) 726-6600

QATAR
Doha
Farig Bin Omran
Tel. 864701

ROMANIA
Bucharest
Str. Tudor Arghezi 7-9
Tel. (0) 10-40-40

RUSSIA
Moscow
Ulitsa Chaykovskogo 19/21/23
Tel. (7) (095) 252-2450

SAUDI ARABIA
Riyadh
Collector Road M.
Tel. (1) 488-3800

SINGAPORE
Singapore
30 Hill Street
Tel. 338-0251

SOUTH AFRICA
Pretoria
225 Pretoria Street
Tel. (12) 28-4266

SPAIN
Madrid
Calle Serrano 75
Tel. (1) 276-3400

SUDAN
Khartoum
Sharia Ali Abdul Latif
Tel. 74700

SWEDEN
Stockholm
Strandvagen 101
Tel. (8) 783-53-00

SWITZERLAND
Bern
Jubilaeumstrasse 93
Tel. (31) 437011

SYRIA
Damascus
Rue Al-Mansur 2
Tel. (11) 33-3052

TAIWAN
Taipei
Hsin Yi Road
Tel. (2) 7092000

TAJIKISTAN
Dushanbe
#39 Ainii Street
Tel. (7) (3772) 24-32-23

THAILAND
Bangkok
95 Wireless Road
Tel. (2) 2525040

TUNISIA
Tunis
144 Avenue de la Liberté
Tel. (1) 78-25-66

TURKEY
Ankara
110 Ataturk Bulvari
Tel. (4) 126-54-70

TURKMENISTAN
Ashkhabad
Yubilenaya Hotel
Tel. (7) (3630) 24-49-26

UKRAINE
Keiv
#10 Vul. Yuriy Kotsubinskoho
Tel. (7) (044) 244-7349

UNITED ARAB EMIRATES
Abu Dhabi
Al-Sudan Street
Tel. (2) 336691

UNITED KINGDOM
London
24 Grosvenor Square
Tel. (1) 499-9000

URUGUAY
Montevideo
Lauro Miller 1776
Tel. (2) 23-60-61

UZBEKISTAN
Tashkent
#55 Chelendarskaya
Tel. (7) (3712) 77-14-07

VENEZUELA
Caracas
Avenida Miranda & Floresta
Tel. (2) 285-3111

YUGOSLAVIA
Belgrade
Kneza Milosa 50
Tel. (11) 645-655

APPENDIX 4

Foreign Embassies and Chanceries in Washington, D.C.

(Area Code 202)

AFGHANISTAN, DEMOCRATIC REPUBLIC OF
2341 Wyoming Avenue, NW, 20008   234-3770

ALGERIA, DEMOCRATIC AND POPULAR REPUBLIC OF
2118 Kalorama Road, NW, 20008   265-2800

Iranian Interests Section
2209 Wisconsin Avenue, NW, 20007   965-4990

ANTIGUA AND BARBUDA
3400 International Drive, NW, #2H, 20008   362-5122

ARGENTINE REPUBLIC
1600 New Hampshire Avenue, NW, 20009   939-6400

ARMENIA
122 C Street, Suite 360, 20001   628-5766

AUSTRALIA
1601 Massachusetts Avenue, NW, 20036   797-3000

AUSTRIA
2343 Massachusetts Avenue, NW, 20008   483-4474

BAHAMAS, COMMONWEALTH OF THE
600 New Hampshire Avenue, NW, Suite 865, 20037   944-3390

BAHRAIN, STATE OF
3502 International Drive, NW, 20008   342-0741

BANGLADESH, PEOPLE'S REPUBLIC OF
2201 Wisconsin Avenue, NW, 20007   342-8372

BARBADOS
2144 Wyoming Avenue, NW, 20008   939-9200

BELGIUM
3330 Garfield Street, NW, 20008   333-6900

BELIZE
3400 International Drive, Suite 2J, NW, 20008   363-4505

BENIN, PEOPLE'S REPUBLIC OF
2737 Cathedral Avenue, NW, 20008   232-6656

BOLIVIA
3014 Massachusetts Avenue, NW, 20008   483-4410

BOTSWANA, REPUBLIC OF
4301 Connecticut Avenue, NW, Suite 404, 20008   244-4990

BRAZIL
3006 Massachusetts Avenue, NW, 20008   745-2700

BRUNEI
2600 Virginia Avenue, NW, Suite 300, 20037   342-0159

BULGARIA, PEOPLE'S REPUBLIC OF
1621 22nd Street, NW, 20008   387-7969

BURKINA FASO
2340 Massachusetts Avenue, NW, 20008   332-5577

BURMA (See MYANMAR)

BURUNDI, REPUBLIC OF
2233 Wisconsin Avenue, NW, Suite 212, 20007　　　342-2574

CAMEROON, REPUBLIC OF
2349 Massachusetts Avenue, NW, 20008　　　265-8790

CANADA
501 Pennsylvania Avenue, NW, 20001　　　682-1740

CAPE VERDE, REPUBLIC OF
3415 Massachusetts Avenue, NW, 20007　　　965-6820

CENTRAL AFRICAN REPUBLIC
1618 22nd Street, NW, 20008　　　483-7800

CHAD, REPUBLIC OF
2002 R Street, NW, 20009　　　462-4009

CHILE
1732 Massachusetts Avenue, NW, 20036　　　785-1746

CHINA, PEOPLE'S REPUBLIC OF
2300 Connecticut Avenue, NW, 20008　　　328-2500

COLOMBIA
2118 Leroy Place, NW, 20008　　　387-8338

**COMOROS, FEDERAL ISLAMIC
REPUBLIC OF**
336 East 45th, 2nd Floor
New York, NY 10017　　　(212) 972-8010

CONGO, PEOPLE'S REPUBLIC OF
4891 Colorado Avenue, NW, 20011　　　726-5500

COSTA RICA
1825 Connecticut Avenue, Suite 211, NW, 20009　　　234-2945

CÔTE D'IVOIRE
2424 Massachusetts Avenue, NW, 20008　　　797-0300

CUBA (See CZECHOSLOVAKIA)

CYPRUS, REPUBLIC OF
2211 R Street, NW, 20008   462-5772

CZECHOSLOVAK SOCIALIST REPUBLIC
3900 Linnean Avenue, NW, 20008   363-6315

Cuban Interests Section
2630 and 2639 16th Street, NW, 20009   797-8518

DENMARK
3200 Whitehaven Street, NW, 20008   234-4300

DJIBOUTI, REPUBLIC OF
1430 K Street, Suite 600, NW, 20006   347-0254

DOMINICAN REPUBLIC
1715 22nd Street, NW, 20008   332-6280

ECUADOR
2535 15th Street, NW, 20009   234-7200

EGYPT, ARAB REPUBLIC OF
2310 Decatur Place, NW, 20008   232-5400

EL SALVADOR
2308 California Street, NW, 20008   265-3480

EQUATORIAL GUINEA
801 Second Avenue, Suite 1403
New York, NY 10017   (212) 599-1523

ESTONIA
630 Fifth Avenue, Suite 2415
New York, NY 10111   212-247-0499

ETHIOPIA
2134 Kalorama Road, NW, 20008   234-2281

FIJI
2233 Wisconsin Avenue, NW, Suite 240, 20007   337-8320

FINLAND
3216 New Mexico Avenue, NW, 20016 — 363-2430

FRANCE
4101 Reservoir Road, NW — 944-6000

GABON
2034 20th Street, NW, 20009 — 797-1000

GAMBIA, THE
1030 15th Street, NW, Suite 720, 20005 — 842-1356

GERMANY, FEDERAL REPUBLIC OF
4645 Reservoir Road, NW, 20007 — 298-4000

GHANA
3512 International Drive, NW, 20008 — 686-4520

GREECE
2221 Massachusetts Avenue, NW, 20008 — 667-3168

GRENADA
1701 New Hampshire Avenue, NW, 20009 — 265-2561

GUATEMALA
2220 R Street, NW, 20008 — 745-4952

GUINEA, REPUBLIC OF
2112 Leroy Place, NW, 20008 — 483-9420

GUINEA-BISSAU, REPUBLIC OF
211 East 43rd Street, Suite 604
New York, NY 10017 — (212) 661-3977

GUYANA
2490 Tracy Place, NW, 20008 — 265-6900

HAITI
2311 Massachusetts Avenue, NW, 20008 — 332-4090

HOLY SEE
3339 Massachusetts Avenue, NW, 20008 — 333-7121

HONDURAS
3007 Tilden Street, NW, 20008   966-7702

HUNGARY, REPUBLIC OF
3910 Shoemaker Street, NW, 20008   362-6730

ICELAND
2022 Connecticut Avenue, NW, 20008   265-6653

INDIA
2107 Massachusetts Avenue, NW, 20008   939-7000

INDONESIA, REPUBLIC OF
2020 Massachusetts Avenue, NW, 20036   775-5200

IRAN (See ALGERIA)

IRAQ
1801 P Street, NW, 20036   483-7500

IRELAND
2234 Massachusetts Avenue, NW, 20008   462-3939

ISRAEL
3514 International Drive, NW, 20008   364-5500

ITALY
1601 Fuller Street, NW, 20009   328-5500

JAMAICA
1850 K Street, NW, Suite 355, 20006   452-0660

JAPAN
2520 Massachusetts Avenue, NW, 20008   939-6700

JORDAN, HASHEMITE KINGDOM OF
3504 International Drive, NW, 20008   966-2664

KENYA
2249 R Street, NW, 20008   387-6101

KOREA, REPUBLIC OF
2370 Massachusetts Avenue, NW, 20008   939-5600

KUWAIT, STATE OF
2940 Tilden Street, NW, 20008   966-0702

LAO PEOPLE'S DEMOCRATIC REPUBLIC
2222 S Street, NW, 20008   332-6416

LATVIA
4325 17th Street, NW, 20011   726-8213

LEBANON
2560 28th Street, NW, 20008   939-6300

LESOTHO, KINGDOM OF
2511 Massachusetts Avenue, NW, 20008   797-5534

LIBERIA, REPUBLIC OF
5201 16th Street, NW, 20011   723-0437

LITHUANIA
2622 16th Street, NW, 20009   234-5860

LUXEMBOURG
2200 Massachusetts Avenue, NW, 20008   265-4171

MADAGASCAR, DEMOCRATIC REPUBLIC OF
2374 Massachusetts Avenue, NW, 20008   265-5525

MALAWI
2408 Massachusetts Avenue, NW, 20008   797-1007

MALAYSIA
2401 Massachusetts Avenue, NW, 20008   328-2700

MALI, REPUBLIC OF
2130 R Street, NW, 20008   332-2249

MALTA
2017 Connecticut Avenue, NW, 20008   462-3611

MARSHALL ISLANDS, REPUBLIC OF THE
Suite 1004, 1901 Pennsylvania Avenue, NW, 20006

MAURITANIA, ISLAMIC REPUBLIC OF
2129 Leroy Place, NW, 20008   232-5700

MAURITIUS
4301 Connecticut Avenue, NW, Suite 134, 20008   244-1491

MEXICO
1911 Pennsylvania Avenue, NW, 20006   728-1600

MICRONESIA
706 G Street, SE, 20003   544-2640

MOROCCO
1601 21st Street, NW, 20009   462-7979

MOZAMBIQUE, PEOPLE'S REPUBLIC OF
1990 M Street, NW, Suite 570, 20037   293-7146

MYANMAR, UNION OF
2300 S Street, NW, 20008   332-9044

NEPAL
2131 Leroy Place, NW, 20008   667-4550

NETHERLANDS, THE
4200 Linnean Avenue, NW, 20008   244-5300

NEW ZEALAND
37 Observatory Circle, NW, 20008   328-4800

NICARAGUA
1627 New Hampshire Avenue, NW, 20009   387-4371

NIGER, REPUBLIC OF
2204 R Street, NW, 20008   483-4224

NIGERIA
2201 M Street, NW, 20037   822-1500

NORWAY
2720 34th Street, NW, 20008   333-6000

OMAN, SULTANATE OF
2342 Massachusetts Avenue, NW, 20008   387-1980

PAKISTAN, ISLAMIC REPUBLIC OF
2315 Massachusetts Avenue, NW, 20008   939-6200

PAPUA NEW GUINEA
1330 Connecticut Avenue, NW, 20036   659-0856

PARAGUAY
2400 Massachusetts Avenue, NW, 20008   483-6960

PERU
1700 Massachusetts Avenue, NW, 20036   833-9860

PHILIPPINES
1617 Massachusetts Avenue, NW, 20036   483-1414

POLAND, REPUBLIC OF
2640 16th Street, NW, 20009   234-3800

PORTUGAL
2125 Kalorama Road, NW, 20008   328-8610

QATAR, STATE OF
600 New Hampshire Avenue, NW, Suite 1180, 20037   338-0111

ROMANIA
1607 23rd Street, NW, 20008   232-4747

RUSSIAN FEDERATION
1125 16th Street, NW, 20036   939-8907

RWANDA, REPUBLIC OF
1714 New Hampshire Avenue, NW, 20009   232-2882

SAINT KITTS AND NEVIS
2501 M Street, NW, Suite 540, 20037   833-3550

SAINT LUCIA
2100 M Street, NW, Suite 309, 20037   463-7378

SAO TOME AND PRINCIPE
801 Second Avenue, Suite 1504, NY 10017   (212) 697-4211

SAUDI ARABIA
601 New Hampshire Avenue, NW, 20037   342-3800

SENEGAL, REPUBLIC OF
2112 Wyoming Avenue, NW, 20008   234-0540

SEYCHELLES, REPUBLIC OF
820 Second Avenue, Suite 927, NY 10017   (212) 687-9766

SIERRA LEONE
1701 19th Street, NW, 20009   939-9261

SINGAPORE, REPUBLIC OF
1824 R Street, NW, 20009   667-7555

SOMALI DEMOCRATIC REPUBLIC
600 New Hampshire Avenue, NW, Suite 710, 20037   342-1575

SOUTH AFRICA
3051 Massachusetts Avenue, NW, 20008   232-4400

SPAIN
2700 15th Street, NW, 20009   265-0190

SRI LANKA, DEMOCRATIC SOCIALIST REPUBLIC OF
2148 Wyoming Avenue, NW, 20008   483-4025

SUDAN, REPUBLIC OF THE
2210 Massachusetts Avenue, NW, 20008   338-8565

SURINAME, REPUBLIC OF
4301 Connecticut Avenue, Suite 108, NW, 20008   244-7488

SWAZILAND, KINGDOM OF
3400 International Drive, NW, 20008   362-6683

SWEDEN
600 New Hampshire Avenue, NW, Suite 1200, 20037   944-5600

SWITZERLAND
2900 Cathedral Avenue, NW, 20008   745-7900

SYRIAN ARAB REPUBLIC
2215 Wyoming Avenue, NW, 20008   232-6313

TANZANIA, UNITED REPUBLIC OF
2139 R Street, NW, 20008   939-6125

THAILAND
2300 Kalorama Road, NW, 20008   483-7200

TOGO, REPUBLIC OF
2208 Massachusetts Avenue, NW, 20008   234-4212

TRINIDAD AND TOBAGO
1708 Massachusetts Avenue, NW, 20036   467-6490

TUNISIA
1515 Massachusetts Avenue, NW, 20005   862-1850

TURKEY, REPUBLIC OF
1714 Massachusetts Avenue, NW, 20036   659-8200

UGANDA, REPUBLIC OF
5909 16th Street, NW, 20001   726-7100

UKRAINE
2001 L Street, NW, Apt. 200, 20036   452-0939

UNITED ARAB EMIRATES
600 New Hampshire Avenue, NW, Suite 740, 20037   338-6500

**UNITED KINGDOM OF GREAT BRITAIN AND
NORTHERN IRELAND**
3100 Massachusetts Avenue, NW, 20008   462-1340

URUGUAY
1918 F Street, NW, 20006   331-1313

VENEZUELA
2445 Massachusetts Avenue, NW, 20008   797-3800

WESTERN SAMOA, INDEPENDENT STATE OF
820 Second Avenue
New York, NY 10017   (212) 599-6196

YEMEN ARAB REPUBLIC
600 New Hampshire Avenue, NW, Suite 840, 20037   965-4760

YUGOSLAVIA, SOCIALIST FEDERAL REPUBLIC OF
2410 California Street, NW, 20008   462-6566

ZAIRE, REPUBLIC OF
1800 New Hampshire Avenue, NW, 20009   234-7690

ZAMBIA, REPUBLIC OF
2419 Massachusetts Avenue, NW, 20008   265-9717

ZIMBABWE
2852 McGill Terrace, NW, 20008   332-7100

COMMISSION OF THE EUROPEAN COMMUNITIES
2100 M Street, NW, Suite 707, 20037   862-9500

APPENDIX 5 ⌇

U.S. State Department Passport Agencies

Boston Passport Agency
Thomas P. O'Neill Federal Building
10 Causeway Street, Room 247
Boston, MA 02222
*Recording: (617) 565-6998
Public Inquiries: (617) 565-6990

Chicago Passport Agency
Kluczynski Federal Building
230 South Dearborn Street, Suite 380
Chicago, IL 60604-1564
*Recording: (312) 353-5426
Public Inquiries: (312) 353-7155 or 7163

Honolulu Passport Agency
New Federal Building
300 Ala Moana Boulevard, Room C-106
Honolulu, HI 96850
*Recording: (808) 541-1919
Public Inquiries: (808) 541-1918

Houston Passport Agency
Concord Towers
1919 Smith Street, Suite 1100
Houston, TX 77002
*Recording: (713) 653-3159
Public Inquiries: (713) 653-3153

Los Angeles Passport Agency
11000 Wilshire Boulevard, Room 13100
Los Angeles, CA 90024-3615
*Recording: (213) 209-7070
Public Inquiries: (213) 209-7075

Miami Passport Agency
Federal Office Building, 16th Floor
51 SW First Avenue
Miami, FL 33130-1680
*Recording: (305) 536-5395 (English)
(305) 536-4448 (Spanish)
Public Inquiries: (305) 536-4681

New Orleans Passport Agency
Postal Services Building, Room T-12005
701 Loyola Avenue
New Orleans, LA 70113-1931
*Recording: (504) 589-6728
Public Inquiries: (504) 589-6161

New York Passport Agency
Rockefeller Center
630 Fifth Avenue, Room 270
New York, NY 10111-0031
*Recording: (212) 541-7700
Public Inquiries: (212) 541-7710

Philadelphia Passport Agency
Federal Office Building, Room 4426
600 Arch Street
Philadelphia, PA 19106-1684
*Recording: (215) 597-7482
Public Inquiries: (215) 597-7480

San Francisco Passport Agency
525 Market Street, Suite 200
San Francisco, CA 94105-2773
*Recording: (415) 974-7972
Public Inquiries: (415) 974-9941

Seattle Passport Agency
Federal Office Building
915 Second Avenue, Room 992
Seattle, WA 98174-1091
*Recording: (206) 442-7941
Public Inquiries: (206) 442-7945

Stamford Passport Agency
One Landmark Square
Broad and Atlantic Streets
Stamford, CT 06901-2767
*Recording: (203) 325-4401
Public Inquiries: (203) 325-3538 or 3530

Washington, D.C. Passport Agency
1425 K Street, NW
Washington, DC 20524-0002
*Recording: (202) 647-0518
Public Inquiries: (202) 647-0518

---

* The twenty-four-hour recording includes general passport information, passport agency location, and hours of operation.

APPENDIX 6

U.S. Customs Offices in the United States

Regional Offices—United States Customs Service

Regional Headquarters/ District Offices	Address
NATIONAL HEADQUARTERS: Washington, DC	1301 Constitution Avenue, NW
NEW YORK: New York, NY	6 World Trade Center, 10048
	Kennedy Airport, 11430
Newark, NJ	Airport International Plaza, 07114
NORTH CENTRAL: Chicago, IL	55 East Monroe Street, 60603
	610 South Canal Street, 60607
Cleveland, OH	55 Erie View Plaza, 44114
Detroit, MI	477 Michigan Avenue, 48226

Duluth, MN	209 Federal Building, 55802
Great Falls, MT	600 Central Plaza, 59401
Milwaukee, WI	517 East Wisconsin Avenue, 53202
Minneapolis, MN	110 South 4th Street, 55401
Pembina, ND	Post Office Building, 58271
St. Louis, MO	7911 Forsyth Building, 63105

NORTHEAST:

Baltimore, MD	40 South Gay Street, 21202
Boston, MA	10 Causeway Street, 02222
Buffalo, NY	111 West Huron Street, 14202
Ogdensburg, NY	127 North Water Street, 13669
Philadelphia, PA	2nd and Chestnut Streets, 19106
Portland, ME	312 Fore Street, 04112
Providence, RI	24 Weybosset Street, 02903
St. Albans, VT	Main and Stebbins Streets, 05478

SOUTH CENTRAL:

Mobile, AL	150 Wall Street, 36652
New Orleans, LA	423 Canal Street, 70130

SOUTHEAST:

Charleston, SC	200 East Bay Street, 29401
Miami, FL	909 SE 1st Avenue, 33131
	77 SE 5th Street, 33131
Norfolk, VA	101 East Main Street, 23510
San Juan, PR	U.S. Customhouse (PO Box 2112), 00903
Savannah, GA	1 East Bay Street, 31401
Tampa, FL	4430 East Adams Drive, 33605

| Washington, DC | PO Box 17423, 20041 |
| Wilmington, NC | 1 Virginia Avenue, 28401 |

SOUTHWEST:

Dallas/ Fort Worth, TX	700 Parkway Plaza, Dallas/Fort Worth Airport, 75261
El Paso, TX	Bridge of the Americas, PO Box 9516, 79985
Houston, TX	5850 San Felipe Street, 77057
Houston/ Galveston, TX	701 San Jacinto Street, 77052
Laredo, TX	Lincoln-Juarez Bridge, 78041
Nogales, AZ	International and Terrace Streets, 85621
Port Arthur, TX	4550 75th Avenue, 77642

PACIFIC:

Anchorage, AK	620 East 10th Avenue, 99501
Honolulu, HI	335 Merchant Street, 96806
Los Angeles, CA	300 North Los Angeles Street, 90053
Los Angeles/ Long Beach, CA	300 South Ferry Street, San Pedro, CA 90731
Portland, OR	511 NW Broadway, 97209
San Diego, CA	880 Front Street, 92188
San Francisco, CA	555 Battery Street, 94126
Seattle, WA	909 1st Avenue, 98174

APPENDIX 7 ⌒

Visa Services

A Travisa
   2122 P Street, NW
   Washington, DC 20037
   (202) 463-6166

All Points Visa, Inc.
   4900 Auburn Avenue
   Suite 201
   Bethesda, MD 20814
   (301) 652-9055

Ambassador Visa
   2025 I Street, NW
   Suite 806
   Washington, DC 20006
   (202) 728-6701

Atlas Visa Services
   2341 Jefferson Davis Highway
   Arlington, VA 22202
   (703) 521-6400

**Center for International
   Business and Travel**
   2135 Wisconsin Avenue, NW
   Suite 400
   Washington, DC 20007
   (202) 333-5550

DMS Visa International
   1611 Connecticut Avenue,
   NW
   Suite 1
   Washington, DC 20009
   (202) 745-3815

Deran Visa Service
1701 Wind Haven Way
Vienna, VA 22180
(703) 281-4743

Duke's Visa Service
2033-A 38th Street, SE
Washington, DC 20020
(202) 582-0280

Embassy Visa Service
2162 California Street, NW
Washington, DC 20008
(202) 387-1171

Express Visa Service
2150 Wisconsin Avenue, NW
Washington, DC 20007
(202) 337-2442

Globetrotters
935 South Buchanan Street
Arlington, VA 22204
(703) 522-2999

Nader Visa Service, Inc.
1325 18th Street, NW
Washington, DC 20036
(202) 332-7797

Visa Advisors
1808 Swann Street, NW
Washington, DC 20009
(202) 797-7976

Wakay Visa Services, Inc.
1519 Connecticut Avenue,
NW
Washington, DC 20036
(202) 337-0300

**Washington Visa and Travel
Document Center**
2025 I Street, NW
Washington, DC 20006
(202) 452-0999

Zierer Visa Service
1521 New Hampshire
Avenue, NW
Suite 100
Washington, DC 20036
(202) 265-3007

APPENDIX 8 ～

U.S.A. Direct Local Numbers

Calling the United States from overseas is fast and easy with AT&T U.S.A. Direct Service. You may talk to an AT&T operator in the United States and use your AT&T card or call collect.

Dial Access Countries (dial from any phone in these countries):

Argentina   001-800-200-111
Aruba   800-1011
Australia   0014-881-011
Austria†   022-903-011
Bahamas²   1-800 872-2881
Bahrain   800-001
Belgium   11-0010
Brazil   000-8010
British Virgin Islands   1 800 872-2881
Cayman Islands   1872
Chile   00*-0312
Colombia²   980-11-0010
Costa Rica†   114
Czechoslovakia   00-420-00101
Denmark†   8001-0010

Dominica   1 800 872-2881
Dominican Republic   1 800 872-2881
Finland†   9800-100-10
France†   19*-0011
Gambia†   001-199-220-0010
Germany[1]   0130-0010
Greece†   00-800-1311
Grenada[2]   872
Guam[2]   018-872
Guatemala†   190
Hong Kong   008-1111
Hungary†   00*-36-0111
Indonesia   00-801-10
Italy†   172-1011
Jamaica[2]   0 800 872-2881
Japan†   0039-111
South Korea   009-11
Liberia   797-797
Macau   0800-111
Netherlands†   06*-022-9111
Netherlands Antilles   001-800-872-2881
New Zealand   000-911
Norway†   050-12-011
Panama   109
Peru[2]   ##0
Philippines†[2]   105-11
Singapore†   800-0011
Saint Kitts   1 800 872-2881
Sweden†   020-795-611
Switzerland†   046-05-0011
United Kingdom   0800-89-0011
Uruguay†   00-0410

Designated Telephone Countries. U.S.A. Direct Service is available only from specially marked telephones in major airports, hotels, cruise ports, telephone centers, and on U.S. military bases and fleet centers in these countries: Antigua, Argentina, Aruba, Bahamas, Bahrain, Barbados, Belize, Bermuda, British Virgin Islands, People's Republic of China, Colombia, Costa Rica, Dominican Republic, Ecuador, Egypt, El Salvador, Ghana, Guam, Guatemala, Haiti, Honduras, Hong Kong, India, Indonesia, Israel, Italy, Jamaica, Japan, South Korea, Liberia, Malaysia, Mexico, Netherlands Antilles, Panama, Philippines, Spain, Saint Lucia, Suriname, Taiwan, Thailand, Trinidad and Tobago, Turks and Caicos, Venezuela

A. For more information about AT&T U.S.A. Direct Service, call 1-800-874-4000 ext. 359 or call collect at 412-553-7458 from overseas. To report U.S.A. Direct Service problems, call 1-800-222-3000 from the U.S.

B. With U.S.A. Direct Service, use your regular AT&T card number (the large number in the center), not the international number.

---

* Await second dial tone.
† Public phones require coin or card.
1 Trial basis only.
2 Limited availability.

APPENDIX 9

Airline Clubs

Certain airlines provide lounges for their first and business class passengers at no added cost. The amenities offered in each club and lounge vary according to airline and location.

LOUNGES OR CLUBS WITH MEMBERSHIP
FEE OR FLYING REQUIREMENT

Alaska Airlines - Boardroom

Requirements: Membership fee

Locations: Anchorage, Seattle, Portland, San Francisco, Los Angeles

Telephone: 1-800-426-0333

Address: Alaska Airlines
The Boardroom
PO Box 68900
Seattle, WA 98168

Alitalia - VIP Lounge

Requirements: No membership fee, but passenger must fly a certain number of miles per year

Locations:	Milan, New York (La Guardia)
Telephone:	1-800-221-4745
Address:	None specific to the lounges

American Airlines - Admirals Club

Requirements:	Membership fee
Locations:	Atlanta, Austin, Bogota, Boston, Buenos Aires, Chicago, Cleveland, Dallas/Fort Worth, Denver, Detroit, Frankfurt, Honolulu, Kansas City, Lima, London (Gatwick/Heathrow), Los Angeles, Miami, Nashville, New York (JFK/La Guardia), Orange County, Paris, Philadelphia, Raleigh/Durham, St. Louis, San Diego, San Francisco, San Jose, San Juan, Santo Domingo, Seattle, Toronto, Washington, D.C. (Dulles/National)
Telephone:	1-800-433-7300
Address:	American Airlines Admirals Club PO Box 620081 Dallas, TX 75262-0081

America West - Phoenix Club

Requirements:	Membership fee
Locations:	Orange County, Phoenix (2)
Telephone:	1-800-247-5691 (general) 602-220-4072 or 273-2994 (Club in Phoenix) 714-252-6168 (Club in Orange County)
Address:	Phoenix Club Administration 4000 Sky Harbor Boulevard Phoenix, AZ 85034

British Airways - Executive Club

Requirements:	Free presently, but normally membership fee
Location:	Dallas
Telephone:	1-800-955-2748
Address:	British Airways Executive Club PO Box 660361 Dallas, TX 75266-0361

Continental Airlines - Presidents Club

Requirements: Membership fee

Locations: Chicago (O'Hare), Denver, Cleveland, Honolulu, Newark, Phoenix, Seattle, Los Angeles, London (Gatwick), San Francisco, Houston Intercontinental

Telephone: 1-800-435-0040

Address: Presidents Club
770 Lexington Avenue
New York, NY 10021

Delta Airlines - Crown Room Club

Requirements: Membership fee

Locations: Anchorage, Atlanta, Birmingham, Boston, Calgary, Chicago (O'Hare), Cincinnati, Dallas/Fort Worth, Denver, Detroit, Fort Lauderdale, Honolulu, Jacksonville, Las Vegas, Los Angeles, Memphis, Miami, Minneapolis/St.Paul, Nashville, Newark, New Orleans, New York (La Guardia), Orlando, Portland, Raleigh/Durham, Sacramento, San Antonio, San Francisco, Salt Lake City, Seattle, Tampa, Vancouver, West Palm Beach, Washington, D.C.

Telephone: 1-800-221-1212

Address: Delta Airlines
Crown Room Club Membership Center
Department 857
PO Box 20533
Atlanta, GA 30320-2533

Lufthansa - Senator Lounge

Requirements: Free to ticketed first class travelers; any passenger is eligible for a Senator card by producing over $25,000 of revenue per year

Locations: Bangkok, Bombay, Boston, Bremen, Buenos Aires, Cologne, Düsseldorf, Hamburg, Hanover, Hong Kong, London (Heathrow), Los Angeles, Mexico City, Munich, New York (JFK), Nuremberg, Osaka,

Paris, Philadelphia, Rio de Janeiro, San Francisco, Stuttgart, Tokyo, Washington, D.C., Vienna, Zurich

Telephone: See below

Address: See below

Lufthansa Frequent Traveler Lounge

Requirements: Free to ticketed business class passengers, or to passengers producing a certain amount of revenue per year

Locations: Cologne, Düsseldorf, Frankfurt, Hamburg, Hanover, Munich, New York (JFK), Nuremberg, Stuttgart

Telephone: 1-800-645-3880

Address: Lufthansa German Airlines
Washington Dulles International
PO Box 17703
Washington, DC 20041

Northwest Airlines - WorldClubs

Requirements: Membership fee

Locations: Bangkok, Boston, Chicago (O'Hare), Cleveland, Detroit, Hong Kong, Honolulu, London (Gatwick), Los Angeles, Manila, Memphis, Milwaukee, Minneapolis/St.Paul, New York (JFK/La Guardia), Osaka, Phoenix, San Francisco, Seattle/Tacoma, Seoul, Taipei, Tampa, Tokyo (Narita), Washington, D.C. (National)

Telephone: 1-800-225-2525

Address: Northwest Airlines
WorldClubs Service Center, Department C6330
Minneapolis/St.Paul, MN 55111-3075

TWA - Ambassadors Club:

Requirements: Membership fee

Locations: Albuquerque, Boston, Columbus, Dayton, Kansas City, Los Angeles, Madrid, Milan, Newark, New York (JFK/La Guardia), Paris, Phoenix, Pittsburgh,

Rome, St. Louis, San Francisco, Washington, D.C. (Dulles/National), West Palm Beach, Dallas, Frankfurt, London (Gatwick-Centennial Suite)

Telephone: 1-800-527-1468

Address: TWA Ambassadors Club
PO Box 27-459
Kansas City, MO 64180

United Airlines - Red Carpet Club

Requirements: Membership fee

Locations: Auckland, Baltimore, Bangkok, Boston, Chicago, Denver, Hong Kong, Honolulu, London (Heathrow), Los Angeles, Manila, Melbourne, Newark, New York (La Guardia), Osaka, Philadelphia, Pittsburgh, Portland, San Francisco, Seattle, Seoul, Sydney, Taipei, Tokyo (Narita), Washington, D.C. (National/Dulles)

Telephone: 1-800-722-5243

Address: United Airlines
Red Carpet Club
PO Box 92880
Los Angeles, CA 90009-9900

US Air - US Air Club:

Requirements: Membership fee

Locations: Baltimore, Boston, Buffalo, Charlotte, Cleveland, Dayton, Greensboro, Hartford/Springfield, Indianapolis, Los Angeles, Newark, New York (La Guardia), Orlando, Philadelphia, Phoenix, Pittsburgh, Raleigh/Durham, Rochester, San Diego, Rochester, San Diego, Syracuse, Tampa, Washington, D.C. (National)

Telephone: 1-800-828-8522

Address: The US Air Club
P.O. Box 641170
Pittsburgh, PA 15264-1170

LOUNGES WITH NO MEMBERSHIP FEES

These lounges are free for all first and business class passengers.

Air Canada - MapleLeaf Lounge

Requirements: Also free to elite members of Air Canada's frequent flyer Airoplan, or to holders of an en route gold business card affiliated with Air Canada

Locations: Los Angeles, Calgary, Chicago, Edmonton, Fredericton, Halifax, London (Ontario), Miami, Moncton, New York (La Guardia), North Bay, Ottawa, Regina, St. John's, San Francisco, Saskatoon, Sidney, Sudbury, Tampa, Thunder Bay, Timons, Toronto, Montreal, Vancouver, Victoria, Winnipeg

Telephone: 1-800-361-8253

Address: None specific to the lounges

Air New Zealand - Koru Club

Locations: Auckland, Christchurch, Honolulu, Los Angeles, Wellington, Melbourne, Singapore, Tokyo; access to other clubs in Cairns, Frankfurt, London (Gatwick), Sydney

Telephone: 1-800-262-1234

Address: None specific to the lounges

Ana-All Nippon Airways - Lounge

Locations: Bangkok, London, New York (JFK), Washington, D.C. (Dulles), Los Angeles, Tokyo (Narita)

Telephone: 1-800-235-9262

Address: None specific to the lounge

Austrian Airlines - VIP Lounge

Requirements: No membership fee. Open to first and business class passengers

Locations: Located everywhere they fly except Johannesburg, South Africa

Telephone: 1-800-843-0002

Address: None specific to the lounges

Canadian Airlines - Empress Lounge

Locations: Amsterdam, Auckland, Bangkok, Beijing, Buenos Aires, Calgary, Copenhagen, Edmonton, Frankfurt, Halifax, Hong Kong, Honolulu, London (Gatwick), Los Angeles, Manchester, Milan, Montreal, Munich, Ottawa, Paris, Rio, Rome, St. John's, San Francisco, San Paulo, Tokyo, Toronto, Vancouver, Winnipeg

Telephone: 1-800-426-7000

Address: None specific to the lounges

Quantas Airlines - Captains Club

Requirements: Free to business and first class passengers

Locations: Located everywhere they fly; facilities vary

Telephone: 1-800-227-4500

Address: Customer Relations Manager
                      360 Post Street
                      San Francisco, CA 94108

APPENDIX 10 ⤳

Airline Meals

All special meal requests are made through the reservations number (at least twenty-four hours in advance).

American Airlines: 1-800-433-7300. The number for the Admirals Club is 1-800-237-7971.

British Airways: 1-800-247-9297. The number for the Executive Club is the same.

Air France: 1-800-237-2747. The number for Club 2000 is 1-800-237-2746.

Delta Airlines: 1-800-221-1212. The number for the Crown Room Club is the same.

Lufthansa Airlines: 1-800-645-3880. Special clubs are arranged by calling the local airport. In Washington, D.C., the number is 202-296-5604.

Trans World Airlines: There is *no* 800 number for TWA. The traveler must call the local airport. In Washington, D.C. the number is 202-833-1000. The same applies to the Ambassadors Club. In Washington, D.C. the number is 202-833-1000.

United Airlines: Like TWA, United has no 800 number. The traveler must call the local airport. In Washington, D.C. the number is 703-742-4600. The number for the Red Carpet Club in Washington, D.C. is 703-892-7655.

Bibliography

Axtell, Roger E. *Do's and Taboos around the World*. New York: John Wiley and Sons, 1990.

———. *Do's and Taboos of Hosting International Visitors*. New York: John Wiley and Sons, 1990.

Bartlett, Christopher A., and Sumantra Ghoshal. *Managing across Borders*. Cambridge, MA: Harvard Business School Press, 1989.

Berris, Jan Carol. "The Art of Interpreting." In *Intercultural Communication, A Reader*, 6th ed., edited by Larry A. Samovar and Richard E. Porter. Belmont, CA: Wadsworth Publishing Company, 1991.

Binnendijk, Hans, ed. *International Negotiating Styles*. Washington, DC: Foreign Service Institute, 1987.

———. *National Negotiating Styles*. Washington, DC: Foreign Service Institute, 1987.

Braganti, Nancy L., and Elizabeth Devine. *European Customs and Manners*. New York: Simon and Schuster, 1992.

———. *The Traveler's Guide to Latin American Customs and Manners*. New York: St. Martin's Press, 1989.

Chambers, Kevin. *The Traveler's Guide to Asian Customs and Manners*. New York: Simon and Schuster, 1988.

Ehret, Charles F., and Lynne Waller Scanlon. *Overcoming Jet Lag.* New York City: Berkley Publishing Co., 1986.

Fisher, Glen. *International Negotiation.* Yarmouth, ME: Intercultural Press, 1980.

Fitzgerald, John E., and Charles M. Saggio. *Frequent Flyer Award Book.* Lincolnwood, IL: National Textbook, 1987.

Hall, Edward T., and Mildred R. Hall. *Understanding Cultural Differences: Germans, French and Americans.* Yarmouth, ME: Intercultural Press, 1989.

Hill, Deborah J. *Travel Tips International.* Frederick, CO: Renaissance House Publishers, 1990.

Kohls, L. Robert. *Survival Kit for Overseas Living.* Yarmouth, ME: Intercultural Press, 1984.

McDonald, Roger. *The Breakaway Guide to Trouble-Free Travel.* London: British Broadcasting Corporation and the British Automobile Association, periodically revised.

Rearwin, David. *The Asia Business Book.* Yarmouth, ME: Intercultural Press, 1991.

Ricks, David A. *Big Business Blunders: Mistakes in Multinational Marketing.* Homewood, IL: Dow Jones-Irwin, 1983.

Rossman, Marlene L. *The International Businesswoman: A Guide to Success in the Global Marketplace.* New York: Praeger Publishers, 1986.

Sakmar, Thomas P. *Health Guide for International Travelers.* Lincolnwood, IL: National Textbook, 1986.

Shames, Germaine W. and Glover, W. Gerald. *World Class Service.* Yarmouth, ME: Intercultural Press, 1989.

Snowdon, Sandra. *The Global Edge: How Your Company Can Win in the International Marketplace.* New York: Simon and Schuster, 1986.

Storti, Craig. *The Art of Crossing Cultures.* Yarmouth, ME: Intercultural Press, 1990.

Terpstra, Vern. *The Cultural Environment of International Business.* Cincinnati: South-Western Publishing, 1978.

Other Resources

GENERAL

American Express Travelers Companion. Available free from American Express offices. Contains addresses of all overseas American Express offices and other information.

Background Notes. Available from Superintendent of Documents, U.S. Government Printing Office, Washington, DC 20402.

Business America. Published biweekly by the U.S. Department of Commerce. Available from Superintendent of Documents, U.S. Government Printing Office, Washington, DC 20402.

Buyer Beware: Guidelines Governing Restrictions on Imports of Wildlife into the United States. Available free from Publications Unit, U.S. Fish and Wildlife Service, Department of the Interior, Room 130, Arlington Square, 1849 C Street, NW, Washington, DC 20240.

Consumer Reports Travel Letter. Write to Subscription Department, Consumer Reports Travel Letter, Box 5136B, Boulder, CO 80321-1366.

Crisis Abroad—What the State Department Does. Available free from CA/PA, Room 5807, Department of State, Washington, DC 20520. Summarizes the work done by the State Department during a crisis, including the efforts it makes to obtain reliable information from local authorities abroad for concerned relatives and friends of Americans located in troubled areas.

Foreign Visa Requirements. U.S. State Department publication available from Consumer Information Center, Department 438T, Pueblo, CO 81009.

Health Information for International Travel. Available from Superintendent of Documents, U.S. Government Printing Office, Washington, DC 20402.

Traveling Healthy. A newsletter devoted to travel and health; published six times a year. Available from Traveling Healthy, 108-48 70th Road, Forest Hills, NY 11375; 718-268-7290.

Health Guide for International Travelers. By Thomas P. Sakmar. National Textbook Co., Lincolnwood, IL, 1986.

Key Officers of Foreign Service Posts. Available from Superintendent of Documents, U.S. Government Printing Office, Washington, DC 20402. Updated three times yearly.

Know Before You Go: Customs Hints for Returning U.S. Residents. Available free from any local customs office or from U.S. Customs Service, PO Box 7407, Washington, DC 20044.

Tips. This is a series available free from the Bureau of Consumer Affairs, Public Affairs Staff, Room 5807, Department of State, Washington, DC 20530. Send self-addressed, stamped envelope with your request. Countries/regions for which *Tips* are available include the Caribbean, Cuba, Eastern Europe, Mexico, the Middle East, People's Republic of China, USSR, and Saudi Arabia.

Trip Tips on Bringing Food, Plant and Animal Products into the United States. Available free from the Animal and Plant Health Inspection Service, U.S. Department of Agriculture, 732 Federal Building, 6505 Belcrest Road, Hyattsville, MD 20782.

VEHICLE IMPORTATION

For information on requirements for importing vehicles, contact the U.S. Department of Transportation, 400 7th Street, SW, Room 6115, Washington, DC 20590. For the EPA's rules and regulations, contact the U.S. Environmental Protection Agency, Manufacturer's Operations Division (EN-340F), Investigations/Imports Section, 401 M Street, SW, Washington, DC 20460; 202-382-2504.

- A "gas guzzler" tax may be levied on your vehicle. These taxes range from $500 to $3,850 per vehicle. For more information contact Internal Revenue Service, Public Affairs Office, 1111 Constitution Avenue, NW, Washington, DC 20224.
- The State of California has its own program for regulating the importation of nonconforming vehicles that are sold, registered, or operated in California. For more information on California's requirements contact State of California, Air Resources Board, Multisource Control Division, 9528 Telstar Avenue, El Monte, CA 91731.
- Your state may have its own requirements for nonconforming vehicles. For more information contact your state's Department of Motor Vehicles before you buy.

FEAR OF FLYING

Books

White Knuckles. Lane Ridley. New York: Doubleday, 1987, $5.95.

Freedom from Fear of Flying. Captain T. W. Cummings. Pocketbooks, $3.95.

Videocassettes

Freedom from Fear of Flying. Captain T. W. Cummings, 2021 Country Club Prado, Coral Gables, FL 33134, $25.

Soar (Seminars on Aero Anxiety Relief). PO Box 747, Westport, CT 06881; 800-332-7359; three-set volume, $285.

Help for Fearful Flyers. PO Box 4097, Alexandria, VA 22303; 703-671-7680, $29.95.

Seminars

"Achieving Flight." Dr. Reid Wilson, North Carolina; 919-942-0700, $295.

"Soar." Various airports, $165.

"Freedom from Fear of Flying." Captain T. W. Cummings, 2021 Country Club Prado, Coral Gables, FL 33134; four three-hour sessions, $300.

"Open Skies." Dr. Diana Ronnell, Boston, MA; 617-491-1296, $300.

"Pegasus Fear of Flying Seminar." PO Box 7155, Watchung, NJ 07060; 800-237-8400; ext. 359, $320.

"Round House Square Phobia Treatment Center Fearless Flying Program." 1444 Duke Street, Alexandria, VA 22314; 703-836-7130; five two-hour classes, $285.

"The Phobia Center of Dallas/Ft. Worth." 4307 Newton, Suite 11, Dallas, TX 75219; 214-522-6181; a two-weekend series of classes, $595.

"US Air's Fearful Flyers Program." PO Box 100, Glenshaw, PA 15116; 412-486-5917 (various cities); seven sessions, $250.

"Fear Of Flying Clinic." 1777 Borel Place, Suite 300, San Mateo, CA 94402; 415-341-1595; series of sessions, $450.

Pamphlets

"Phobia Society of America." 133 Rollins Avenue, Suite 4B, Rockville, MD 20852-4004; 301-231-9350 (send a postcard requesting free booklet on phobias and list of resources for particular locales).

SHORT-TERM INSURANCE POLICIES
FOR TRAVELERS

- The International Airline Passengers Association (IAPA), Box 660074, Dallas, TX 75266; 800-527-5888.
- International Travelers Association, 1100 17th Street, NW, Washington, DC 20036; 301-652-3150.
- International Underwriters/Brokers, Inc., 1029 Investment Building, 1511 K Street, NW, Washington, DC 20005; 800-237-6615.
- Travel Assistance International, 1133 15th Street, NW, Suite 400, Washington, DC 20005; 202-347-2025.
- The Travelers Insurance Company, One Tower Square, Ticket and Travel Department, Hartford, CT 06183; 800-243-3174.
- Travel Guard International, 1100 CenterPoint Drive, Stevens Point, WI 54481; 800-782-5151.

ORGANIZATIONS PROVIDING
FOREIGN CURRENCY TRAVELER'S CHECKS

American Express; 800-221-7282

Bank of America; 800-227-3460

Barclays; 800-221-2426

Citicorp; 800-645-6556

Thomas Cook; 800-223-2131

Visa; 800-227-6811

CREDIT CARD EMERGENCY NUMBERS

American Express Green Card; 800-327-2177

American Express Gold Card; 202-783-7474

Diners Club or Carte Blanche; 800-525-9135

MasterCard; 314-275-6100

Visa; 703-827-8400

Visa Premiere; 415-570-3200